The Bible:
A Sustaining Presence in Worship

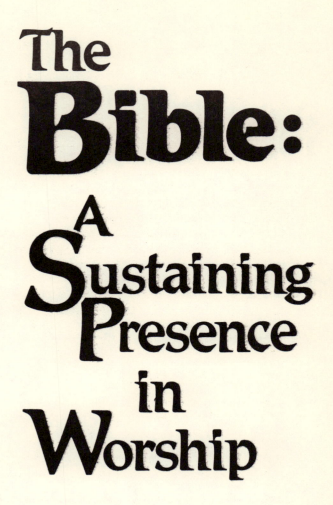

The Bible: A Sustaining Presence in Worship

William H. Willimon

Judson Press® Valley Forge

THE BIBLE: A SUSTAINING PRESENCE IN WORSHIP

Copyright © 1981
Judson Press, Valley Forge, PA 19481

Library of Congress Cataloging in Publication Data

Willimon, William H.
  The Bible, a sustaining presence in worship.

  Includes bibliographical references.
  1. Public worship. 2. Worship—History—Early church, ca. 30-600. 3. Bible. N.T.—Theology.
I. Title.
BV15.W53   264'.34   81-8301
ISBN 0-8170-0918-3   AACR2

The name JUDSON PRESS is registered as a trademark in the U.S. Patent Office.
Printed in the U.S.A. ⊕

And they devoted themselves to the apostles'
teaching and fellowship, to the breaking of
bread and the prayers. *Acts 2:42*

To

HELENA PITTS

of
The Broad Street United Methodist Church
Altar Guild

How that woman loves to worship!

Contents

Introduction

One of the major forces in contemporary liturgical renewal is the rediscovery that the Bible—in its origin, canonization, and traditional usage—is a book of *worship*. The biblical testimony is muted when read in a private, detached fashion. It thrives within a living, worshiping community of faith. We must not forget that we are dealing with an intensely public and communal product. In our present individualistic, fragmented situation it is easy to forget that the Bible was written to be read aloud within the context of the church's worship. The Word is best heard, interpreted, and understood by those who respond to the Word in worship. Without the sustaining presence of the Bible in our services, our worship is severed from its roots, cast adrift, unable to judge whether the God it worships is the God of Abraham, Isaac, Jacob, and Jesus—or only a false god whom we have created for ourselves.

In worship and preaching the Word does not simply bless and confirm the present state of the worshiping community. The sustenance that the Bible offers the church is forever a judging, critical, prodding presence among us. Many of our accustomed worship practices, many of the current attitudes with which we approach worship and preaching, are judged inadequate and even unfaithful when held up to the canons of Scripture. Therefore, recovery of the Bible in our worship has not only meant the recovery of our primary content in worship but also the rediscovery of our most persistent critic.

In other words, the Bible—especially the New Testament—is in constant dialogue with the church's worship, sometimes inspiring and affirming us, sometimes criticizing and prodding us. This book is an attempt to sensitize pastors, seminarians, and other worship leaders and preachers to some of the practical fruits of that dialogue. I make no attempt to be systematic in my treatment of New Testament liturgical themes, nor could I hope, in a book of this scope, to present all possible themes. Once again, the Bible is not a book *about* worship or a book that merely *contains* some worship material. It is a book *of* worship—throbbing throughout with the beat of the people's raucous praise and heartfelt prayers, still dripping with the cleansing waters, still tasting bread and wine upon its lips as it proclaims the Good News that God's presence is among God's people. That book, that product of the gathering of the faithful who came before us, both sustains and judges the gathering of the faithful today.

Chapter 1 is an overview of the role of the New Testament in our present worship as well as the worship practices of the New Testament. Chapter 2 answers the question, "Why worship?" by speaking of worship as Doxology. Prayer and the gift of worship are the concerns of chapter 3. The next chapter deals with data on the Lord's Supper in Luke–Acts. Then baptism is examined from the standpoint of a major biblical interpretation of the rite. Biblical preaching is the subject of chapter 6. Christian worship as the transforming and healing vision and Christian work as dependent upon that vision are the concerns of the next chapter's study on the Transfiguration. Finally, the week-to-week rhythm of worship as the primary means of God's sustaining presence is reflected upon, using the biblical concept of blessing and relating it to blessing in worship.

My thanks to the students and faculty of Duke Divinity School who gave me guidance in these thoughts, especially my colleagues in biblical studies at Duke: Drs. Frank Young, James Efird, and Moody Smith. Inspiration for this book was provided by the good folk of Northside United Methodist Church in Greenville, South Carolina, whom I led in worship while I wrote.

Reformation Sunday, 1980

1

The Bible and Worship

1 CORINTHIANS 11:23

I begin this book with some general thoughts about biblical worship. That phrase, "biblical worship," can be used in at least two ways. We may mean by "biblical worship" the use of the Bible within Christian worship. We then might examine ways in which the Bible can be used to guide and form our worship today. On the other hand, we might mean by "biblical worship" worship in Bible times, assuming that how the people in biblical times praised God can inform and reform how we praise God today. If this were our meaning, we would then examine the Bible, looking for traces of liturgies, hymns, prayers, and forms of worship within the Bible.

This book is a fledgling attempt to do both things. It deals with biblical worship both as a phenomenon of the early church and of the church today. There can be no "biblical worship" today without some knowledge of what worship was like then. On the other hand, the Bible is not a mere history book to be studied and picked apart in an abstract, objective way. It is a book of prayer, proclamation, and praise, which only makes sense within the context of a living community of prayer, proclamation, and praise. In fact, one could argue that the present lethargic, detached state of much biblical criticism could be attributed to biblical scholarship's withdrawal from the church to the safer and more detached confines of academia. But that is another sermon.

Because this book is concerned both with what New Testament worship was then and with what New Testament worship is today, I shall introduce the following thoughts about worship by stating my overriding assumptions about these two dimensions.

A Strange Silence

A look at the average Sunday service today in the average Protestant church reveals, in the words of James D. Smart, a "strange silence of the Bible in the church."[1] The Bible is not read in the worship of most Protestant churches in any systematic way. The Old Testament is often omitted altogether. Thus, the preacher recanonizes Scripture to suit his or her own taste. When bits and pieces of the New Testament are read, they function mainly as a textual springboard for an often unbiblical sermon. This relative silence of Scripture is surprising, particularly when it is within those churches who pride themselves in being "biblical" churches. We Protestants are supposed to be people of the Book, followers of the Word. But the average Methodist, Baptist, or Presbyterian church would be put to shame in its treatment of Scripture by the worship of the average Roman Catholic church—which reads three lessons every Sunday. The problem is not limited only to our public reading of Scripture. How often are our public prayers, confessions, and hymns shaped and guided by scriptural images and metaphors? All too many free-church prayers and hymns have forsaken biblical imagery in favor of a host of frivolous, superficial, pop psychological jargon and clichés that chatter about "celebration," "becoming human," "finding ourselves," "being free to be you and me," and other amorphous trivialities. This is particularly tragic among those whose forebears once felt that the presence and guidance of Scripture in worship was something worth dying for.

A recent informal survey of the worship practices within my own denomination (United Methodist) revealed that as many as 20 percent of the churches surveyed sometimes read *no* Scripture lessons on Sunday morning. Another 30 percent said that, more than likely, the only Scripture they would read next Sunday would come from one of the Gospels. Not only is Scripture not read in worship, but it also does not inform the content of the service. The result of this divorce of Sunday worship from the Bible is often a frothy "celebration" of the congregation's life together at that moment in time or an assertion of its vague, common belief in some kind of God somewhere who wants the congregants to do something. On Easter there is talk of butterflies and daisies rather than the empty tomb and the cross. On Christmas the congregation is treated to readings from *The Velveteen Rabbit.* Folk songs from the "Top Forty" record charts replace the church's psalms. Warm fuzzies, good feelings, ethical platitudes, pep rallies for various social crusades or denominational programs replace attempts to wrestle with God's program. Rather than calling such worship idolatry or apostasy, all too many of us label it "contemporary" and "relevant." At least no one calls it faithful.

Fortunately, the tide seems to be turning. The most important new books on preaching have stopped talking about sermons being multimedial, exciting, entertaining, dialogical, and shocking and are once again concerned with preaching being biblical. Leander Keck's *The Bible in the Pulpit* and D. Moody Smith's *Interpreting the Gospels for Preaching*[2] are outstanding examples. Among our seminarians, there is a new seriousness about the recovery of the Bible in the pulpit. We are now dealing with a generation that has been subjected to Power-of-Positive-Thinking pablum from liberal Protestant pulpits or else the smiling God-loves-you platitudes of the twice-born television preachers. Now—having discovered that this brand of preaching wears thin when subjected to the hard facts of life in the late twentieth century—people are searching for a higher and more radical authority. In their search they are entering again what has been described as "the strange new world of the Bible."

In this book I hope to complement, in an introductory and preliminary way, current attempts to recover the Bible in preaching by attempting to recover the Bible in worship. I will examine various aspects of our present worship from New Testament points of view. Near the end of this chapter (see the section "Worship in the New Testament") I will designate various liturgical materials within the New Testament. But for now I want to suggest some specific, practical ways in which we Protestant worship leaders can recover the Bible within our Sunday worship.

The first and most obvious thing we must do is, fortunately, the easiest. *We must read the Bible within our services.* When we read the Bible in public, aloud, we are coming close to the same speaking and listening dynamic out of which the Bible was born. In contrast to silent reading, speaking the text aloud brings the present congregation back to the way the Bible spent its first thousand plus years—as a word spoken aloud to those who listen. This spoken word is always more direct, personal, and engaging than the silently read word. Public reading is the average person's main contact with the Bible. It is not too much to ask churches to follow the historic practice of reading three lessons every Sunday—Old Testament, epistle, and Gospel.

Whenever I say this, preachers invariably ask, "Am I supposed to preach from all three lessons?" Of course not. In fact, the attempt to construct a sermon from three separate lessons usually results in the distortion of the witness of each lesson in a futile attempt to harmonize the lessons. While it is utterly essential for us to recover truly biblical preaching—preaching that takes a text and humbly, skillfully, openly listens to the text and lets it speak for itself—it is also essential simply to *read* the Word. It is as important to hear the Word as to hear words about the Word.

A wonderful aid in opening up the riches of the Word for God's people is the use of one of the new lectionaries that has been cooperatively constructed by Roman Catholics, Episcopalians, Presbyterians, United Methodists, Lutherans, members of the United Church of Christ, and others.[3] Use of a lectionary is a time-honored practice of the church, which allows us to treat a wide range of Scripture in fairly orderly, progressive fashion. Lectionaries provide Old Testament, epistle, and Gospel lessons for every Sunday of the year. The new lectionaries are on a three-year cycle that allows for the public reading of all four Gospels in their entirety, most of the Epistles, and a significant portion of the Old Testament. The historic rationale for using a lectionary is that God's people ought to hear God's Word—whether a sermon is preached from that Word or not.

For preachers who follow the discipline of lectionary-based preaching, wonderful opportunities are available for systematic, in-depth biblical preaching. The lectionary allows us to preach from all the Gospels and many of the Epistles in depth because we are preaching from a *lection continua,* reading each book from beginning to end. When we preach from one book for several months, we can deal with it in depth. The lectionary disciplines us to read and preach from vast portions of the Old Testament that we have long neglected. There are now more homiletical study aids for lectionary-based preaching than have been available in the entire history of Christian preaching.[4] By using these resources, every preacher can utilize the insights of the latest and best contemporary biblical scholarship.

When the lectionary guides worship leaders and planners, it is possible to construct the Sunday service on the basis of the appointed lessons for the day since most of the lessons follow a general theme or are linked together by a common concern or image in the Gospel. We are able to select hymns, offer prayers, and preach sermons on the basis of Scripture rather than the preacher's whims or some new program that the denomination happens to be pushing on a given Sunday. By allowing the lessons to guide us in our planning, services are given coherence, an orderly progression, and a theological grounding that will help solve some of the problems we currently have on Sunday morning.

Also, by using the lectionary preachers and worship planners know which Scripture will be read far enough in advance so that we can do long-range planning of music and sermons, months or even years in advance. Church musicians have long complained that whereas the average church choir prepares music months in advance, the musician does not know what the Sunday Scripture or sermon will be until a few days before the service. We can offer our congregations new opportunities for Bible study related to the read and preached Word on Sunday morning. The congregation can study the appointed lesson at home before the texts are read and preached from the following Sunday. Church school curriculum materials and Bible study groups can be coordinated to study the lessons also. This can be a wonderful way to involve people in both reading and interpreting the Bible.

A few practical suggestions: The Bible belongs on the pulpit. The adoption of the "divided chancel" a few years ago in some Protestant churches, with a pulpit on one side of the church and a lectern with Bible on the other, tended to confuse visually the relationship between the Bible and preaching. The biblical Word must be integrally linked to the preached word. The preached word is dangerously adrift when it is not grounded in the biblical Word. The biblical Word can be dismissed as irrelevant and archaic when it is not enlivened and applied in the preached word. The "Word of God—word of man" dichotomy is a false separation. God has not ceased speaking to God's people with the closing of the canon. The canon itself is not some pristine gift from on high. When the Bible is preached and interpreted, it is not being tampered with dangerously. It is both returning to the primal, oral experience in which it was born and extending itself into the living present.

The pulpit Bible should be a substantial, finely bound book that is large enough to be visible to the congregation. No paperback, shoddy looking, or pocket testaments belong in the pulpit. The Protestant habit of preaching with a small, personal Bible clutched to one's chest or flopped open in the palm of one hand is a sentimental habit that is a poor symbol of the role of Scripture in preaching. This is the *community's* book, not the preacher's private possession. When the Bible is read, the pages should be turned as the reader moves from one text to the next. Announcing chapter and verse numbers before reading a lesson is unnecessary if the congregation already has the texts printed in their bulletins. It is enough to say, "The Lesson from Isaiah" or "The Word of God as found in the Gospel of Mark."

In public reading of Scripture no paraphrased or colloquial versions of the Bible (such as *The Living Bible*) should be used. A reliable translation in formal, contemporary English (Revised Standard Version, *The New English Bible, The Jerusalem Bible*) is best.

We should be as careful and skillful in our Bible reading as we are in our preaching. We must read distinctively and in a manner that conveys both the liveliness and the importance of the words we are reading. Lay readers should be invited to read some or all of the lessons. In fact, in many congregations there may be lay persons who are more skillful and more gifted public readers than the pastor. These lay persons should be entrusted with the reading of Scripture on Sunday. But no one should serve as lector unless that person has first practiced reading the lessons aloud and has received sufficient instruction in public reading.

When reading three lessons, especially if they happen to be long lessons, it is good to intersperse the lessons with hymns, anthems, or sung congregational response. This is an ancient practice of the church. I also like to give a brief introduction to the lessons, such as, "In today's lesson, Paul writes to a bitterly divided church at Corinth, a church torn apart by jealousy and self-righteousness. This is what he says. . . ." or "The Hebrews have at last made it to the Promised Land. Now they need guidance in how to live in that land. Hear God's word to them. . . ."

After the lessons are read, the reader may wish to lift up the Bible and say, "The Word of God" or give some other visible gesture or sign to show love and respect for the Bible. In the Church of Scotland, the sexton solemnly carries the Bible in at the beginning of the service, places it upon the pulpit and opens it as the pastor and the congregation stand in silence. This act reminds the congregation— and the preacher—that we stand under the sacred Word in our preaching and worship. Some churches have the Bible brought in by a child or teenager when the worship leaders and choir process to their places. (This is a good way to involve younger members in worship leadership.) These gestures and acts help to portray visibly the central place that the Bible occupies in our common life.

When the Bible is read and preached from within the context of Christian worship, we are reminded that *the Bible is the church's book.* It was written, canonized, and interpreted only within the church. The church and its worship came first—then came the church's book. It was written to be read aloud in a group—not silently and individually. In other words, when the Bible is read aloud in public worship, it is not undergoing some strange experience or being placed in some foreign context: The Bible is coming alive within its native habitat where it was born and where it must live if it is to live at all.

This is not to say that the church "owns" the Bible, so to speak. While the Bible is "our" book, it is also our most trenchant and persistent critic. The Bible is the judge of the church in New Testament times and in our day—its judgment includes that of the church's worship. It is the final standard by which all else must be evaluated. Without the correction offered by this biblical judgment, without the continuity with our past which the Bible gives us, the church easily degenerates into a religious club or a social agency designed to fulfill the needs of a transitory clientele. Our worship becomes therapy, or intellectual stimulation, or an aesthetic experience, or a mutual admiration society, or anything else that the culture happens to be buying and peddling at the time. This is not the church. Apart from its Scriptures, the church has no enduring identity as church. Apart from the church, the Scriptures have no enduring context or voice.[5]

The Bible as a Worship Resource

One of the major concerns of contemporary worship renewal is the lack of biblical content in our worship. We have been careless with our speech. Many who previously complained about the problem of archaic biblical language in worship have substituted meaningless contemporary language. As a result, people are bombarded with a host of vague clichés and cute slogans that lack sufficient depth for the seriousness of the divine-human encounter. Thank goodness that worn-out thing called "celebration" has at last grown so vacuous and trite that it has passed from our liturgical vocabulary. There are other nonbiblical words that need to follow it out the back door.

As an example, in our university chapel someone has rewritten the already weak creed of the United Church of Canada in the apparent attempt to remove so-called "sexist" language from this creed. I do not object to the motives; rather, I object to what happened to the language and meaning of the creed when it was rewritten. In the creed are these words:

> He calls us to be his Church:
> to celebrate his presence. . . .

Evidently the revisor of the creed objected to the masculine pronouns "he" and "his" as applied to God in these two lines and rewrote the creed to remove the pronouns. The rewritten creed now reads:

> Who calls us to be in the Church:
> to celebrate life and its fulness. . . .

A great deal was changed—much more than the masculine pronouns. For one thing, there is a qualitative difference between being *God's* Church and being *in* (which implies a kind of institutional membership) *the* Church (which forsakes the image of the church as that body that is possessed and loved by God and wedded to Christ). For another thing, I suspect that "celebrating" (to use that nondescript word) "life and its fulness" is the pagan thing to do when we no longer have the presence of Christ! Celebrating "life and its fulness" is exactly what most of the world is doing already. We certainly don't need the gospel or Christ to help us carry out so banal an enterprise.

The point is that language is important. When we cut ourselves off from the heritage of biblically based language, we are on particularly dangerous ground. It is dangerous because worship is the primary means of transmitting, rehearsing, and enacting the corporate memories of the covenant people. This is one reason why liturgy is inherently conserving and conservative. When our corporate memories are lost, we suffer from the corporate amnesia that afflicts much of the church today. We become victims of every doctrinal wind that blows, easy targets for the latest transitory fad that the culture happens to be peddling at the moment, the subject of religious hucksters who neatly package our basic self-centeredness and call it gospel.

Our Puritan forebears sought to liberate us from exclusive reliance on written, fixed prayers in order that we might be free to pray more contextually and particularly. But today, among the heirs of the Puritans, what began as free *biblical* prayer has degenerated into aimless, hackneyed, cliché-ridden rambling amidst the vagaries of contemporary slogans and catchwords. Our Protestant forebears could afford to be "free" in their worship practices because they were securely yoked to the Book. They lived and prayed "by the Book," so to speak—by *our* Book of books. The Quakers were the most extreme in their rejection of all "outward forms" for prayer. But it is said that if all the Bibles in the world were lost, Quaker leader George Fox could have recited the whole Bible from memory. Fox's prayers were completely free and Spirit-led *biblical* prayers. That is a far cry from the "We just want to thank you so much, Jesus. . . ," or "O Lord, strike us with our need for humane existence and ultimate love. . ." free prayers today. These prayers are enslaved to the values and clichés of contemporary culture. Give me a "jealous God" or a people who "like sheep have gone astray" any day over our current abstract banalities.

Most of the Bible's images are concrete, utterly mundane, and everyday: the lost coin, the lost son, the one small seed. The Bible provides the root metaphors for our liturgical language as well as the narrative framework by which Christians interpret and experience reality. In other words, "our" book, the Bible, both nourishes and judges the content of our prayer and praise in public worship.

Being Biblical Without Being Biblicists

In the seventeenth century a debate raged over precisely how the Bible nourishes and judges Protestant worship. The English Puritans insisted on a biblical warrant for everything done in worship. Because they could find no creeds in Scripture, Puritans rejected creeds in worship. The Anglicans, on the other hand, believed that everything that is not expressly forbidden in Scripture is permissible. Because they could find no prohibition against creeds in Scripture, Anglicans continued to use creeds in worship.

The Puritans were misguided in their insistence upon biblical warrant for all *forms* of worship. They were misguided because, while the Bible is a worship book, so to speak, in that it is to be used within worship, it is not a book on *how* to worship. There are only the briefest sketches of worship patterns found in the New Testament. Rubrics are not a scriptural concern. But while the forms of worship are more a Puritan concern than a biblical concern, the *content* of worship is a continuing New Testament concern. As James White has noted, the Puritans "were dead right in insisting that the *contents* of worship depend upon the corporate memories of the community of faith as recorded in scripture."[6]

Christian worship today can be biblical without being biblicist. The biblical memory must be transmitted and interpreted. Our liturgical theology must be held up to the critical light of Scripture. While this is not a book about the history of the forms of worship within the New Testament, there are some rather interesting bits and pieces of information about New Testament worship practices which should be noted.

Worship in the New Testament

Reliable, identifiable data on worship practices and theology within the New Testament is sketchy and, in most instances, inconclusive. The data does reveal one truth about the worship of the New Testament church: It was rich, multifaceted, and used a variety of forms in a variety of locations.[7]

The book of Acts (2:42, 46; 20:7) mentions instruction, preaching, various kinds of prayer, and "the breaking of bread." From the beginning, pastoral *instruction* seems to have been offered within the context of worship. "The teachings of the apostles" had to be delineated and separated from spurious "false teaching." The nature of early *preaching* can be surmised from examples in Acts. Most of these examples trace the history of salvation from the Old Testament to the present. *Prayers* were free, or spontaneous, as well as fixed—after the fashion of Jewish prayer. The Lord's Prayer and the Aramaic *Maranatha* ("Come, Lord Jesus") are examples or fragments of fixed liturgical prayers.

In the *breaking of bread* we have the roots of our present Holy Communion, or Eucharist (the subject of chapter 4)—that ritualized Christian meal that Paul called the "Lord's Supper." While this meal probably took a variety of forms during the New Testament period, the basic "shape of the liturgy" of the table (as Gregory Dix first called it[8]) is clear from the beginning: the taking of bread and cup, the blessing of bread and cup, the breaking of bread, the giving of bread and cup (cf. Luke 22:7-23; 24:30-31; 1 Corinthians 11:23-26). Scripture reading, preaching, prayer, and supper became the basic form for Sunday gatherings of Christians.

The Pauline epistles indicate other New Testament worship practices within or alongside the basic form. In 1 Corinthians 14:26, Paul mentions psalms, revelation, speaking in tongues, and the interpretation of tongues. By *revelation* is meant the special, prophetic, inspired exposition of the Word (1 Corinthians 14:29, 32)."Speaking in tongues" is enthusiastic, ecstatic speech that must be carefully interpreted and guided lest it become, as it was in Corinth, a cause of division. These ecstatic and spontaneous utterances were practiced alongside fixed liturgical forms, such as *psalms and hymns* (Colossians 3:16; Ephesians 5:19). These were probably regarded as they had been in Judaism—both as free compositions and as repeated parts of the service. Some of the earliest Christian songs may be: Revelation 5:9, 12, 13; 12:10-12; 19:1-2, 6; Ephesians 5:14; 1 Timothy 3:16 as well as Philippians 2:5-11; 2 Timothy 2:11-13; and 1 Peter 3:18-22.

There were also fixed liturgical formulae that were used in the early church's services. Romans 10:10 and Philippians 2:11 are parts of early *confessions of faith.* In addition to these confessions, there are numerous formulae for *benedictions.* These benedictions were used at the beginning of the service ("Grace be with you and peace from God our Father and our Lord and Savior") as well as at the end of the service ("The grace of our Lord be with you all"). These benedictions and their meaning will be discussed in the last chapter. *Doxologies,* acts of praise, were also used in the service and are found throughout the epistles (e.g., Romans 11:36; 2 Corinthians 11:31 *a).* The "Amen," taken from Judaism, is a stereotyped, fixed means of showing the congregation's participation in the liturgy (1 Corinthians 14:16).

The rite that allowed people to participate in these acts of worship was *baptism,* the rite of Christian initiation. There are traces of early baptismal liturgies in the New Testament. The baptismal account in Acts 8:37 shows the candidate making the short confession: "I believe that Jesus Christ is the Son of God." First Peter may contain an early baptismal sermon and early baptismal hymns (1 Peter 2:9-10). A Pauline view of baptism will be discussed in chapter 5. Some of the biblical material cited in that chapter may well have been early baptismal prayers and hymns.

New Testament Worship

Once again, the major concern of this book is not the *how* of New Testament worship but the question of the meaning of that worship. We are concerned with worship *in the spirit of,* or *in the manner of,* the New Testament. In spite of the lack of clear, detailed evidence about the worship practices of the New Testament, we can say some important things in general about the spirit of that worship.

First, the worship of the New Testament was seen as the model, the norm, the clearest expression of a Christian's primary business—not only on Sunday, but for the rest of the week as well. In the New Testament no clear distinction can be made between the purpose of a Christian's Sunday work in worship and the Christian's weekday work in the world. We worship in church on Sunday so that we might be able to worship in the world Monday through Saturday. As C. F. D. Moule says:

. . . the Christians of this period saw the worship of God as the whole purpose of life. They did not worship efficiency or security, regarding divine service on Sunday as a means to such ends: the meaning and end of all life was nothing other than the worship of God.[9]

In other words, there is little point in looking for bits of worship "in" Scripture or in looking for bits of Scripture that have been imported into the early church's worship. For the first Christians worship and work were one piece. Scripture was not merely a collection of noble thoughts, intellectual propositions about God, moral directives for life—Scripture was part and parcel of a Christian's praise and prayer vocabulary. What was said and done on Sunday was neither less nor more worshipful than what was said and done the rest of the week.

Certainly, distinctions are made in the Bible between work and worship. But the distinctions are there merely because we cannot do two things at once. It is therefore helpful to set aside specific times and places—such as the Sunday service—for articulating, accentuating, and recapitulating the relationship to God by which we live all our days.

The favorite New Testament word for worship is *leitourgia,* which literally means "the work of the people." This word reminds us of two things: (1) worship is the people's prayer work, not the clergy's work that the people are to sit back and watch nor something that is optional activity from the people; and (2) worship is *work*—hard, active, disciplined, often painful work—which demands something from us even as it gives something to us.

This work is all that a Christian does. It is the serious day-to-day, everyday business of a faithful life, the business which we do most intentionally on Sundays so that we may do it better on Mondays in order that we might be fit to do it naturally for all eternity. Paul said it best: "Whatever you do, in word or deed, do everything in the name of the Lord Jesus, giving thanks to God the Father through him" (Colossians 3:17).

The Westminster divines (1647) knew this when they began their catechism on the Christian life by declaring that the chief end of humanity is "to glorify God and enjoy him forever."

Finally, worship in the New Testament was work done by the people of God in the presence of God in Christ. The Aramaic prayer *Maranatha* is probably the oldest and one of the most expressive of early Christian prayers. If the Aramaic is divided to read *Marana tha,* it means the imperative "O our Lord, come!" corresponding to the Greek phrase in Revelation 22:20, "Amen. Come, Lord Jesus!"

Bultmann argued that the words may also be divided *Maran atha,* so as to read, "Our Lord has come," or, "Our Lord is coming," as a joyous statement of the present rather than a hopeful plea for the future. (Cf. Philippians 4:15—"The Lord is at hand.")

While *Maranatha* is probably, in its oldest form, a prayer that pleads for the final consummation of God's rule in Christ, both meanings of the phrase are possible, and both meanings express two key facets of New Testament worship. When the first Christians gathered for worship, they gathered as people who lived between the times, in the now and the not yet, in the interim between Christ's first and second comings. They waited. The world still groaned in travail, awaiting the consummation of what Christ had begun in his death, resurrection, and ascension. While they waited, they spoke and sang and prayed; they ate together and baptized new converts, telling all who would listen that God had acted decisively on behalf of the world and that God would finish what had been begun in Christ.

But while they waited, they waited not in the absence of their Lord, but in his presence—his sustaining presence. The Lord was coming, but he had also come. The risen Christ was present in his Body, the church, in its gatherings before the table, in its prayers, praise, preaching, and service. He continued to be known to them "in the breaking of bread" even as the first disciples had known him in their midst at Emmaus (Luke 24:35).

The church, "the Body of Christ," as Paul would put it, was not left bereft to sing its songs alone in a strange land as doleful memorials to a lost leader. Every time those of the church gathered, they felt the risen Christ in the midst of them, doing what he had always done for his disciples: teaching them, nourishing them, giving them vision and hope, encouraging them in their struggles, sustaining them as they both waited for and participated in his kingdom—that kingdom that begins to be formed wherever God's people gather in order that God's people may be ready to be gathered when the kingdom at last comes in fullness and power.

To worship as New Testament Christians today means to gather under both the promise of Christ and the presence of Christ, sustained by both our future hope and our present reality of his Lordship. *Maranatha.*

Whatever was written in former days was written for our instruction, that by steadfastness and by the encouragement of the scriptures we might have hope. . . . that together you may with one voice glorify the God and Father of our Lord Jesus Christ (Romans 15:4-6).

2

Why Worship?

REVELATION 15:3*b*-4

Recently I was asked to speak to a group of youth on the topic "Why Worship?"—which really is not a topic but, rather, a question. I do not know who thinks up such questions. Probably not the youth. I suspect that some adult leader, hoping to make a predictably dull subject like worship sound a bit more exciting, thought up the question in the hope of attracting one or two more teenagers. If my suspicions are correct, I'm afraid the adult was disappointed. First of all, teenagers are not as dense as we give them credit for being. They are usually suspicious of cute questions and not-so-subtle adult attempts to lure them into uninteresting religion under the guise of something else they are supposed to be more interested in—such as questions in general.

Second, if the youth are fairly astute, they will recognize that, as questions go, the question "Why worship?" is a rather silly question. It is one of those questions that, when asked, reveals that the questioner is probably too far gone to understand the answer anyway. When someone asks, "What good is a circus?" one is correct in assuming that the question reveals a stupidity so profound and pathetic that finding a suitable answer to the question is the least of the person's problems.

Ours is an age of pathetic questions.

We have congratulated ourselves for being a generation that "accepts nothing at face value and questions everything." And so we are up to our necks in questions, many of which were not asked by previous generations, not necessarily because they were afraid to ask, but because the answers were considered to be self-evident and therefore the questions were deemed irrelevant. We ask: "Why is it good for me to be concerned about someone else other than myself? Why should I work to contribute something to the larger society? Who says that boys were created to be with girls (and vice versa)? Why is it important for parents to nurture their children? Is honesty always a virtue?"

The widely accepted dictum that "one gets an education not to have all the right answers but to be able to ask the right questions" is true only if one has a pathological need to remain forever uncommitted and irresponsible. Many of us today evoke the image of a free-floating, cowardly Socrates; we drift from place to place asking penetrating questions, gathering interesting information, yet never find a truth worth living for or an answer worth dying for. How can such intellectual and spiritual cowardice be called wise?

The Worship of Me

And so some may ask, "Why worship?" I must confess that my first responses to the question are more questions. Why worship? Why kiss someone you love? (Come up with a good "reason" for that one!) Or, for that matter, why send roses, write sentimental poetry, attempt a moonlight serenade, or put on your best suit? This is all rather ridiculous, useless behavior which, to an outside observer, would not seem to do anyone much lasting good. Of course, that's just the problem: An "outside observer" can hardly judge the meaning or the appropriateness of the crude antics of lovers. It only makes sense, if sense be needed, to those who are actually in love. Worship is much like that.

Another response to the question "Why worship?" might be to answer that one should *not* worship—*unless one has to worship.* I am willing to accept the premise that there are some people who need to worship and there are some people who do not need to worship, just as I am willing to accept the premise that there are some lovers who need to kiss their beloved and there are some lovers who don't. There are probably people who never have anything to shout about, or sing about, or cry about. I'm sure that somewhere there are people who never have an inclination to clap their hands and kick up their heels over anything, just as I'm sure that there are people somewhere for whom life is never so tragic as to lead them to clench their fists and scream, "Why did this happen to me?" And, if this is true, I'm sure that there are even more people whose point of view is such that they never look upon the beauty of a flaming sunset, or the face of a smiling child, or the end of a painful illness and ask quietly, "Why did this happen to me?"

I'll admit I've never had the misfortune of knowing people like these, but I'm willing to accept the premise that people like these may exist. Such existing could hardly be called living. I can understand how such people are scratching their heads in befuddlement and wondering, "Why worship?" One should only kiss someone if you're in love with that person. (Or, better still, if you want to find out if you're in love with him or her.) You should only say, "Thanks," if you have been given a gift. Only "worship" (coming from the Old English, "worth-ship") if you think something in life is worthy and worthwhile. You should only clench your fist and scream, "Why me?" if you think that someone "out there" cares about you and has good reasons in the first place. Above all, therefore, only worship if you must worship.

Of course, our questions do reveal something about us. Invariably, behind the "Why worship?" is the more revealing "What's in it for *me?*" We are interested only if we can be assured of some benefit, some payoff for us. Satirist Tom Wolfe has labeled us the "Me Generation." Christopher Lasch has called us the "narcissistic society." In our "do your own thing" culture all people, experiences, activities are judged on the basis of how well they help, cure, excite, soothe *me.* We are offered a myriad of self-help techniques—weekend marathons, massage, nude bathing, assertiveness training, primal screaming, meditation—all of which promise to do something for our adorable *me.*

In Philip Rieff's *The Triumph of the Therapeutic* a new character type emerges, "psychological man," heir of Freud's opposition to communal restrictions and attachments.[1] Psychological man *uses* the community for his own self-enhancement but feels no commitment to any community. He is the center of value, one who is more interested in being "pleased" than "saved." Satisfaction is his goal more than salvation, self-fulfillment his purpose more than self-investment.

Christian worship is bound to be judged irrelevant in a culture which is unable to see beyond the limited confines of its own nose; which assumes that reality can be adequately described and experienced wholly within the self; which cannot see even the neighbor—much less God—because it is so busy looking at its own vaunted needs and self-authenticated truths; which values things, people, and experiences only for what they can give *me.*

Worship is a countercultural activity in a hedonistic, auto-salvation-oriented, pragmatic, utilitarian society. It is scandalously "useless." Worship serves no more worthy "purpose" than the joy of being with the One who loves and is therefore loved. It ranks somewhere near the top of the list of other "useless" and "purposeless" activities such as singing songs, kissing, giving a gift without expecting anything in return, sitting quietly with a good friend, or doing nothing but watching a winter sunset. Can we really blame those busy, serious folk who look at worship and wonder, "What's in it for *me*?" Their very question answers itself—for someone like them, alas, *nothing.*

Unfortunately, the church, in our never-ending flirtation with our culture (in hopes of luring it into the sanctuary), has ended up being seduced by the culture and turning the sanctuary into a marketplace that peddles anything the culture happens to be buying at the time. When culture is in the market for self-gratification and self-centeredness, we have been all too willing to give it what it thought it wanted. When asked, "Why worship?" we are quick to point out all the valuable benefits of worshiping God. While few enlightened Christians admit to the crudity of expecting God to give them a Mercedes in appreciation for an hour in church, they nevertheless do expect "inspiration" or, at a minimum, "a warm feeling" on Sunday morning. (It is not a Mercedes, but who expects miracles anymore?) Or churches advertise that they are "The Friendliest Church in Town," deciding to peddle fellowship rather than feelings. Or people will be assured that worship is therapeutic ("It helps me make it through the week"), or good for the nerves ("I feel a sort of inner peace after I've been to church"), or stimulating to the intellect ("I like a sermon that makes me think or see something in a new way"), or conducive for the building of a unified congregation ("The more we get together, the happier we'll be"), or a pep rally for the church's latest program ("We're only here this morning to get motivated to serve the world"). The old-time tent revivalist used worship as a "preliminary" to soften up hard-shell sinners for a walk down the sawdust trail. New social activists use worship to soften up hard-shell racists or to moralize about our injustices and thus put everybody on a masochistic guilt trip leading nowhere but more deeply within the self. It's all the same. The focus is on *me,* my feelings, my thoughts, my commitments, my guilt, my needs. I am the center of worship, the focus of a carefully orchestrated series of Sunday morning activities that are designed to do something to or for *me.* We are so busy looking at ourselves no wonder we sometimes miss God.

A Defective Tradition

On Sunday morning we are heirs to a defective worship tradition that reinforces some of the worst aspects of our "Me Generation" mentality. The Protestant Reformers in their worship reforms inherited—even accentuated—an already introspective, heavily penitential liturgy. It was full of apologies for our sinfulness and tedious reiteration of the fact that we are miserable sinners, unworthy to gather up the crumbs under the Lord's table, wayward sheep, unclean, in short—"no damn good." As the old *Book of Common Prayer* confessed:

> We acknowledge and bewail our manifold sins and wickedness, which we, from time to time, most grievously have committed, by thought, word, and deed. . . .

Beginning in the Middle Ages, the original New Testament focus of worship shifted from a proclamation of God's mighty acts for humanity to an enumeration of humanity's sins against God. Liturgy became inverted. We apologized rather than rejoiced. Under the guise of humility before the Almighty we succeeded in removing God from the worship service, replacing God with ourselves—*our* sins, *our* guilt, *our* sorrow, *our* penitence. After abolishing the medieval sacrament of penance, we Protestants turned the Eucharist (meaning "Thanksgiving") into a new sacrament of penance (For what do we have to be thankful, and who is able to help us in our wretched state?) and modeled our Sunday services after one Old Testament image (Isaiah 6:1-8). We began all of our services on our knees with a groveling prayer of confession: "Woe is me, for I am a man of unclean lips and dwell in the midst of a people of unclean lips."

One gets the distinct impression, observing us preachers berating our parishioners from the pulpit (whether for their smoking and drinking or for their racism and sexism) and watching our congregations grovel about on their knees, that if Christ ever stood in the midst of our worship and said, "Rise, your sins are forgiven," we would stone him for blasphemously interrupting our humility! Few gifts of God are more threatening than the gift of forgiveness. One doesn't need a psychiatrist to understand the subtle self-gratification and stubborn pride that lurks behind our Sunday morning humility.

On our knees, with our heads bowed low, we are still looking only at ourselves.

We pastors would be wise, every so often, to spend a moment at the beginning of worship looking out over our assembled congregations and asking, "Why are they here?" I can think of at least a dozen good reasons why they should not be there. Oral Roberts is better looking and usually less boring. The beach or golf courses are more inviting. The folk at the country club are more congenial. Time spent plowing through the Sunday paper or doing chores around the house is more productive. If they are there for recreation, or a concert, or a show, or therapy, or intellectual stimulation, or a service club meeting, or a party, they will be disappointed because, in spite of our best efforts over the years, we in the church do not do those things as well as the world does them. Their time would be better spent watching a television evangelist or teeing off at the golf course or reading the Sunday paper if they are looking for that kind of thing.

Doxology

But perhaps they may be there on Sunday morning, week-in-week-out—in spite of all the good modern reasons for not being there, in spite of all the good modern endeavors that the church does not do well, in spite of all our shortcomings as worship leaders and fellow worshipers—because they are looking for God. Or perhaps they are there because, like Augustine before them, they have the notion that God is looking for them. Perhaps they are there seeking, or more accurately, perhaps they are there hoping to be found. Or perhaps they gather not even for so "useful" a purpose as that. Perhaps they assemble for nothing more than, in the words of the old Calvinists, "to glorify God and enjoy him forever." What more revolutionary, subversive activity could one undertake in this "Me Generation" than to be caught singing a doxology?

For from him and through him and to him are all things.
To him be glory for ever. Amen (Romans 11:36).

If my hypothesis proves correct, then we may need to take care, in planning and leading worship, that the God people meet is the God of Abraham, Isaac, and Jacob—not Aphrodite, Zeus, or Cupid; the Only Begotten of the Father—not an inflated image of ourselves. The question for us "homileticians" is still the one John Wesley asked his traveling preachers when they bragged of their success in winning converts and either angering or pleasing people through their preaching: "But did you offer *Christ*?"

A psychiatrist I know (a lapsed Roman Catholic—but he could just as well be a Baptist, Presbyterian, or United Methodist) tells me that he will go back to church "only when they start talking of God again."

"What do they talk about when you go to church?" I asked.

"Oh, I hear advice on how to be friendly, how to vote, how to have a happy marriage, how to feel better about myself. It's all good advice, but it's not different from the advice I get anywhere else. I don't think I need more advice; certainly I don't need more information; rarely do I know what to do with more exhortation—I can't get it out of my head that I need God."

You know whereof this man speaks.

We may have to listen, in our preaching, more to what the Bible is saying than what *Reader's Digest* or Paul Harvey says. We can let "Dear Abby" give people advice. Our prayers may need to revert to stammering sighs so that we might cleanse ourselves of prayers that are little more than conversations among ourselves about ourselves. Or better still, we need to make better use of the prayers of past saints, listening in on their God-talk, joining in their conversation when we can, until we ourselves have been tutored in the art of speaking to One greater than ourselves. We definitely need to stop chattering about our puny misdeeds or non-deeds and to start proclaiming again the mighty deeds of God. We need to stop worrying about ourselves as we worship—whether what we do looks good or is suitably relevant or makes sense or makes us feel comfortable—and let God start remaking us, and start enjoying the presence of the One whose grace reduces such worries to delightful irrelevance. Doxology—*praise*—is the "purpose" of worship. You will get no more reason for it than that: Praise God from whom all blessings flow!

For sometimes I fear that we turn in on ourselves or else peddle friendliness, inspiration, warm feelings, happiness, intellectual stimulation, aesthetic experience, moral edification, and distribution of interesting information when we feel we no longer have God, when we lose that scandalous New Testament church confidence that the One we long to meet has already come and is waiting to meet us.

We may (and must) carefully plan our worship and strive for quality in our music, environment, and preaching; but ultimately, God gives worship as a gift of his presence. When we sing or say a "Call to Worship" or "Invocation" at the beginning of our services, let us never forget that *we* are the ones who need to be called into his presence, *we* are the ones whose presence needs to be invoked. It is our attention that first must be called forth. *Our* absence, *our* lack of focus, *our* inattentiveness—not God's—are the problems. We do not have to import God into people's lives. God is already there impatiently waiting for them and us, seeking us all, invoking our presence, inviting us to the feast long before we shuffle to the meeting. Was not that what Jesus meant in those stories about the prodigal son and the great banquet? As Leo the Great once said of the Eucharist, it merely "makes conspicuous" what and who is always there if only we were not blind as bats to his presence.

And when we cease being impressed with our whys and wherefores and dare to come, on those good and all-too-rare occasions when we meet, we find that God is already there to give us what we need. Sometimes what we get is not what we expected. Sometimes there is inspiration, assurance, healing, revelation, hope, forgiveness. It is one of those strange ironies that, even as we serve God, sometimes we are the ones who end up being served in this service of worship. But just as often there is judgment, ordinariness, fear, confusion, despair, awe and dread. For remember, we are being met by the Living God, not by our more agreeable false gods. And if you do not wish to risk so threatening and mysterious a presence, then you had best not come to the meeting.

But all "good" that comes from worship, whether it be what we asked for and thought we wanted or what we have spent Monday through Saturday avoiding, is pure by-product. For the main gift we receive is God.

Behind all our wants, our deepest questions, and beyond even our very best answers, we may discover in worship that *that* was what we were wanting all along—or should we say that it was *God* who was inquiring after us, seeking us, wanting us all along, seeking with only one good purpose in mind—that God might meet us, surprise us, love us, and enjoy us forever.

> . . . . For thou alone art holy.
> All nations shall come and worship thee. . . .
> —Revelation 15:4

3

Prayer:
Pharisees and Publicans All

LUKE 18:9-14

When people asked Jesus questions, he often responded to their questions with stories—parables. They asked Jesus about prayer. "Teach us to pray," they said. In answering them, he not only gave them a model prayer but also, in Luke's gospel, told them some stories about prayer—the parable of the unjust judge (Luke 18:1-8) followed by the parable of the Pharisee and the publican (Luke 18:9-14).

We continue our reflections on New Testament worship with reflection upon New Testament prayer. I follow the method of Jesus by telling a story of my own, setting it in the context of Jesus' story of the Pharisee and the publican. Take these stories and my reflection upon them as words about prayer or, more specifically, words about prayers and those who pray them on Sunday morning.

A Saturday Night and a Sunday Morning

It was Saturday night and, having put the last touches on my sermon for the next morning, I settled down for a quiet evening with the family. There was a knock at my door. I opened the door to find a policeman standing on my doorstep.

"Preacher," he said, "could you come with me? Some of your church members have gotten into a big brawl, and the chief thinks you might be able to help us settle them down."

I was aghast. Some of my *church* members? How could this be?

The culprits were one of the leading couples in my church. The policeman drove me across town to where they lived. We arrived at a spectacle of confusion, flashing lights, and policemen pinned down behind their patrol cars while their chief pleaded with someone in the house through his bullhorn.

"Now cut out that shooting, Joe, and you two settle down and come on out. You're going to hurt somebody if you ain't careful," blared the chief's voice across the debris-strewn yard. I could see broken glass and overturned furniture, some inside, some outside of the house. It was an apocalyptic vision of chaos and battle. Another shot rang out from the house, and the chief ducked back down behind his car.

This is no place for a man of the cloth, I thought as I inched my way over to the chief's car.

"How are you doing, Reverend?" the chief asked amiably as I joined him in his improvised bunker.

"Not all that well, at the moment," I replied.

"Joe and his wife are having a little argument, it seems, and it has gotten a bit rough; we thought that maybe you could help us settle them down," said the chief.

"A little argument?" I asked in amazement.

"Yes, they usually have one of these every spring."

"You mean to tell me this has happened before?"

"Oh, sure; it's not all that big a deal. They just seem to let things build up during the winter, and then every spring they let it all out, so to speak."

I was appalled. And to think, two of my "best" *church* members.

No shots or curses came from the house for five or ten minutes and, after repeated attempts by the chief to elicit some response from Joe or his wife, the chief pronounced, "They have probably passed out now. It's safe to go on in and get them."

I accompanied the police into the scene of the heart of battle (at a safe distance) where we found Joe and his wife, just as the chief had predicted, passed out on their living room sofa, a bit bruised, scratched up here and there, but in surprisingly good condition for two battle-weary veterans. By that time, neighbors had arrived and were clearing away the debris and helping the two groggy combatants into bed. The chief led his men back to their cars, saying something about, "Well, that ought to hold them until this time next year."

As for me, I was shocked, disappointed, and angry, but mainly I was embarrassed. I returned home determined to relieve Joe of his church duties as soon as possible. Was this any way for one of my parishioners to act?

The next morning, in the quietness and beauty of church, the chaos and disorder of the evening before seemed far away. As I moved through the worship service, I had hardly given the episode a thought until we came to the offering. I dutifully got the offering plates from their place on the altar and turned to hand them to the head usher. And who should be the head usher on this Sunday? Joe. I nearly passed out when I turned around and saw him standing there, smiling sheepishly, bandages on his bruised hands and a cut under one eye, more or less reverently waiting for the plates; Joe, standing there before me, God, and everybody else. This was more than I could take. The nerve of the man! Had he no pride? Had he no self-respect? Can you imagine someone having the nerve to stand before the altar on Sunday morning after a Saturday night like that?

Had he no pride?

Two People at Prayer

He also told this parable to some who trusted in themselves that they were righteous and despised others: "Two men went up into the temple to pray, one a Pharisee and the other a tax collector. The Pharisee stood and prayed thus with himself, 'God, I thank thee that I am not like other men, extortioners, unjust, adulterers, or even like this tax collector. I fast twice a week, I give tithes of all that I get.' But the tax collector, standing far off, would not even lift up his eyes to heaven, but beat his breast, saying, 'God, be merciful to me a sinner!' I tell you, this man went down to his house justified rather than the other; for every one who exalts himself will be humbled, but he who humbles himself will be exalted" (Luke 18:9-14).

The parable of the Pharisee and the publican is one of those Jesus stories that has been so overworked by generations of us preachers that I fear it has become exhausted by the sheer weight of its familiarity. A thousand times we have heard the smug self-righteous-ness of this Pharisee predictably damned and the touching humility of this publican predictably praised. I can therefore sympathize with my former teacher, Bill Meuhl, who says that, as for him, he has had enough of this publican's perpetually breast-beating, groveling humility and his age-old standing off from the altar and proclaiming of his unworthiness, and now he is ready for the man to relinquish his pious despair and get on with the business at hand.[1] When parables get predictable, they cease being helpful. A joke that has been heard a dozen times before ceases to be a joke. And in parables the joke is usually on us.

Parables do not ask for "understanding"—they seek response. They do not ask to be interpreted—they want to interpret us. A parable does not explain "Why?" It exposes. My response to the parable exposes who I am and who God is. A parable is perverted when we slip into the kind of self-righteous moralizing that exhorts, at the end of a story like the Pharisee and the publican, "Do not become like them." The point is, God help us, we are already "like them," up to our necks in the story, so much so that Jesus' word about "them" is a word about us.

It is interesting to note where we find our places within the parables. We try to take the wrong seats. We are invariably the good little wayward son who comes humbly back home, not the sniveling older brother who puts up such a fuss. We are all those good people who had the wisdom to accept the invitation to the great banquet, not those stupid excuse makers who stayed home. We are that humble publican who bowed in admirable humility, not that smug Pharisee who made such a fool of himself in his pompousness. It is interesting to note where we find our roles in these vignettes of life.

Luke says that Jesus told the parable of the Pharisee and the publican to those who trusted in their own righteousness and despised everybody else. At first glance it has little to do with the parable that precedes it, that of the unjust judge (Luke 18:1-8), except that both parables deal with prayer. If the story about the bothersome widow and the crafty judge was told in order to teach that we should persistently "always pray and not lose heart," then perhaps the parable of the Pharisee and the publican was told in order to teach that persistence in prayer is important, but disposition or stance while praying is also important. These people who trust "in their own righteousness and despise everybody else" I take to mean some of us all of the time and all of us some of the time in prayer. This parable has everybody's name upon it.

"Two men went up into the temple to pray. . . ." They go up, for the temple stood on high ground, to pray. One assumes the regular 3 P.M. sacrifice of the lamb is implied here. No feast day is mentioned. Rather, this was a regular service of corporate worship that anyone could attend. At the service worshipers "draw near" to the altar ("draw near" being a cultic expression in the Old and New Testaments) as the priest sacrifices the afternoon lamb for the sins of Israel while the gathered people pray. The priest enters the holy place, swings some incense, then returns to the steps in front of the altar. With the people now prostrating themselves before the altar, the priest lifts his hands, pronounces a blessing upon the people, and announces that God has accepted the atonement for their sins. As silver trumpets blare forth and a psalm is chanted, the people again prostrate themselves, then rise and return to their homes. This is the context for the story.

Two men go up to the temple to pray, that is, they go to worship. Two men go to worship, one a Pharisee, the other a tax collector. Their posture for prayer is the first thing that attracts our attention. The Pharisee stands "with himself," i.e., he stands by himself, one assumes in a prominent or conspicuous position, yet detached from his fellow worshipers. He stands by himself and, as is the custom, probably prays aloud, speaking under his breath. While the Pharisee prays before the altar, he is careful not to stand too close to what he considers to be the common herd of the "unrighteous." Such virtue as his invariably produces a lonely piety that confirms itself by its standing apart.

The Pharisee's prayer is also revealing. He lists first the sins from which he has refrained, then his good deeds. He not only avoids sin but also does good. Among his good deeds are two works that he is in no way expected to perform: He voluntarily fasts twice a week on Mondays and Thursdays, probably interceding for the people's sins, and he gives tithes of everything that he buys so as to be sure that he uses nothing that has not been tithed before it was purchased.[2] He offers God both his person and his purse, going far beyond the "second mile" in his sacrificial devotion. As Augustine first noted, nowhere is the Pharisee condemned. There is no doubt that here we are dealing with a good man—a *very* good man.

Some commentators have rapped the Pharisee for the self-centeredness, the self-congratulatory attitude of his prayer, the way he assumes that he alone is righteous and everyone else is unrighteous. But the prayer begins with, "I thank thee. . . ." As Jeremias notes, from the evidence here, the Pharisee does indeed seem thankful, recognizing that his virtues are gifts of God.[3] He would not change places with the other worshiper, even though the tax collector may be better off materially than he is. The Pharisee does not even bother God with a string of petitions. Thanksgiving is his only goal. There is thus a curious kind of timidity in this Pharisee's prayer in its lack of petition. Or is it a curious kind of pride, which asks for nothing because it assumes it needs nothing? But all in all, it is a fine prayer, liturgically speaking—good form, well said, theologically appropriate. What fault can be found with this prayer?

The stance and prayer of the publican are equally revealing, especially when juxtaposed with the stance and prayer of the Pharisee. As a "tax collector," the publican had ample opportunity for defrauding the public. In the lore of the day, publicans were not only regarded as little better than common thieves, but they were also lackeys for the despised Roman overlords. They had no civil rights and were shunned by all respectable people. In contrast to the stance of the Pharisee, the publican is found before the altar but "standing far off." He does not venture even to lift his eyes to heaven. Since standing with uplifted hands and with one's eyes open was the usual Jewish posture for prayer, the publican's stance is particularly expressive of his utter humility. He bows his head and beats upon his breast, his heart, the center of all sin, as a sign of deepest contrition.

Like the Pharisee, the publican also stands by himself, but not for the same reason. He stands far off in the loneliness of despair over his sinful condition, whereas the Pharisee stands by himself because of his pride over his righteousness. Jeremias says:

> What follows is no part of the usual attitude in prayer; it is an expression of despair. The man smites upon his heart, wholly forgetting where he is, overwhelmed by the bitter sense of his distance from God. He and his family are in a hopeless position, since for him repentance involves, not only the abandonment of his sinful way of life . . . but also the restitution of his fraudulent gains plus an added fifth. How can he know everyone with whom he has had dealings? Not only is his situation hopeless, but even his cry for mercy.[4]

The publican's prayer is hardly a prayer in the traditional sense of the term. There is no cataloging of thanksgiving or petitions, just the simple, straightforward outburst of an anguished man—"God, have mercy on me, a sinner!" Or, more to the point of the specific cultic context, this might be translated, "God, make atonement for me, a sinner!"

The publican claims nothing but asks everything. He asks God to make him righteous, to "justify" him, in other words, to look favorably upon him. He comes forward with empty hands to ask that which only God can give. Lacking anything to give to God, he asks for a gift from God. There is a curious kind of boldness in this publican's humility.

Then comes the punch line. Jesus says, "I tell you this *publican* went back down to his house after worship justified (righteous, blessed with God's pleasure), not the Pharisee." Jeremias notes that this is the only place in the Gospels where "to justify" is used in a sense similar to that which Paul loves to use it.[5] This is significant, not that we have here an example of Pauline influence, for that could hardly be the case. Rather, it is significant because it indicates that the Pauline "justification by faith" is rooted in the teaching of Jesus. The generalizing conclusion of verse 14, that "everyone who makes himself great will be humbled and everyone who humbles himself will be made great," is probably foreign to the parable itself. It is an independent saying that is found elsewhere (e.g., Matthew 23:12; Luke 14:11) and refers to the age to come rather than to the present. It is an eschatological promise of God's action rather than a moralistic exhortation for our action. By locating it here, Luke tends to take some of the bite from the original parable. The "point" here is not about something that *we* are then to "go and do likewise"; *the point is about something that God is doing to and for us.*

Jesus says two men went up to worship before the altar, one a Pharisee, the other a publican. Two men went back down to their homes. One, the publican, was atoned for, forgiven, justified, blessed. The other, the Pharisee, was not.

The Shock of Grace

What I see here is a shocking picture of us at worship, not a lesson on how to worship, for that would be a moralistic perversion of the story. This is a picture of what we already look like when we worship. This is not some sermonette to which we should respond, "OK, gang, let's get out there and get humble." Such self-conscious, posturing "humility" infects much of our worship already. We do not need any more of that brand of pride. Have you ever *tried* to be humble? Pascal noted that "discourses on humility are a source of pride to the vain and of humility to the humble." In regard to being humble, you either are or you aren't.

The smugness of the proud Pharisee can take many forms. "God, I thank thee that I know my weaknesses, not like other men who blissfully think they are righteous." "God, I thank thee that I don't make a big deal of my religion and pray showy prayers, not like all those religious fanatics." I remind you, the Pharisees were the religious "liberals" of Jesus' day, the up-to-date and "enlightened" ones, practitioners of what they preached, taking care that their sabbath religion determined their weekday ethics. Before we take our place beside the "good guy" in the story (if we so misunderstand the story as to think *either* man is the "good guy"), we should remember that "God, I thank thee. . ." can cover a wide array of *self*-justification. As David Read has even suggested, the "Pharisees" of today may not be like that proud Pharisee who took a prominent place before the altar and congratulated himself for his religiosity. Today's people "who trust in their own righteousness" may be those *outside* the temple precincts who pray, "God, I may not be the best person in the world, but at least I'm not like all those hypocrites in the church."[6]

For like the Pharisee at the altar that afternoon, it is easy for even our best-formed, most well-intentioned prayers of thanksgiving to slip into self-congratulation. Just as even our most noble acts of charity sometimes degenerate into twisted attempts at self-gratification, so even our finest prayers to God sometimes turn in on themselves so that it becomes difficult to tell to whom the prayer is addressed. "God, I thank thee for *me.*" Thanksgiving in November is a fine national holiday, but it rarely has much to say to God. It is mainly a time for national self-praise, pride in our achievements, and satisfaction that we have gotten most of what we think we deserve. The presence or grace of God is not necessary on such occasions.

It is not really God whom we seek on such occasions; so it is rarely God whom we receive. Like the Pharisee, we do not need God's mercy and we find none. We come up with hands clenched and full; so it is understandable why we go back down empty. Invariably, the hard cold truth of worship and prayer is that we get what we ask for.

But remember that Jesus said that publicans also join Pharisees before the altar. It is not suggested that the publican is a more upright person than the Pharisee. On the contrary, his main significance here is that *he is a man without merit.* His sin is so thoroughgoing, his condition so wretched, his future so void of hope, that he stands in complete contrast to his fellow worshiper. He is not here in the drama for us to admire or to emulate. He is a sinful, unrighteous man in the fullest sense of the terms, with no qualifying virtues, not even his breast-beating humility, which is little more than his realistic appraisal of his very real wretchedness.

Not that the Pharisee was without sin. In an ultimate sense both men come up as sinners, unrighteous, even though the nature of their sin may differ. There are knowing and unknowing sinners, and both brands of sinners find their expression in these two men. The only difference between saints who are sinners and sinners who are sinners is a noetic difference. Some sin by stealing and others sin by praying, "God, I thank thee that I am not like other men"—both sin. But the publican knows his sin and that is a rather decisive difference.

In this knowledge he comes up to the altar, without claim, without presumption or pride, like a little child who is caught with crumbs on his face before the rifled cookie jar. There is nothing left for him now but mercy. Was this, I wonder, what Jesus was getting at in his talk about "entering the kingdom of God as a little child"? This is the next thing Luke has Jesus say immediately after the parable of the Pharisee and the publican (Luke 18:15-17). Who is spared from those times in life when we childishly cry out, "Save me! I perish!" or when we revert to infantile wishes and childishly wish for peace on earth, or our past to be forgotten, or our lives to be done over and changed for the better, or our grief to be healed? These are the prayers of children who revert to talking about God as if God were Daddy and cry, "*Abba!* Father, I can't do it myself; you must do it for me." "I can't be good; make me good." "I can't earn your love; take me anyway." *Kyrie eleison!* Jesus noted on a number of occasions that children, harlots, and publicans were first in line for the kingdom of God. This is why.

And if there *are* those who are spared moments of childish, helpless, empty-handed regression such as the publican displayed that afternoon at the temple, then such people may never pray as children and therefore never know parental grace. Such self-sufficient adults get what they ask for, and it is rarely God.

But at those times when we come up with hands dirty but also open and empty, without pride and without much of a prayer, the strange thing is that we often go back home with clean hands and full hearts. It is strange and surprising that such publicans as we could come away from the presence of so righteous a God, ourselves made righteous. Grace is always a shocker.

The Gifts of God

I think this parable is about prayer. Not so much about Pharisees and publicans like us who pray prayers as about the One who hears prayers. Jesus says that before any altar of God, in any service of worship, you mainly find two sorts of folk—Pharisees and publicans. A few of us are one or the other all of the time. But most of us are some of both some of the time. We are always torn between the pride of defiance and the pride of despair. There are times when we enter to worship as Pharisees who ask nothing and get nothing. We go home to Sunday dinner with a gnawing emptiness, unjustified and unblessed. Perhaps our trouble was that we were too full (of ourselves?) to receive anything while there. There are also times in life when we enter as publicans, needing everything and return home with more than we dared to ask.

In other words, sometimes we fail at prayer and sometimes we succeed. It is not for us to know when we will go back home "made righteous." All we know (according to Luke's preceding parable of the unrighteous judge) is that we are to keep at it. The gift of righteousness, atonement, justification is only God's to give. It is not surprising that we should come back from worship empty-handed because we usually come with hands so full. Grace is not grace if it is expected. Sometimes it is there for us and sometimes it is not.

Why?

Jesus does not answer that one in this parable. The gift is God's to give out of the unreasonableness of his unfathomable mercy. In spite of what we teachers of worship might lead you to believe, Christians do not go back home righteous and justified because we have prayed correctly, or done it all in proper fashion, or struck a sufficiently humble stance. If we be justified, if we be blessed, if our worship and prayer "work," it is only as a *gift* of God's love. His mercy is without bounds, extending to sinners of all kinds and their well-said or half-blurted-out prayers. It is only through the mercy that we ever return home from church any different than we came. Only through the mercy.

No, Joe, I would not have been caught dead up there before the altar, before God and all the righteous that Sunday morning after your kind of Saturday night. You see, I am too good for that kind of imprudence in worship. It's bad form. I must keep my distance from such as you. I have too much pride to bear my bandaged and still bleeding wounds before the altar, smiling sheepishly, holding out my bruised knuckles as if I were expecting to be given some gift. I have my pride. I have my pride.

Two men went up to the temple to pray, one a Methodist preacher, the other a wife-beating, drunken lout. . . . the latter went back down to his house justified, not the former.

4

The Lord's Supper:
Memories of Meals

LUKE 22:14-38

Every time the family of God (the church) gathers for worship, one of the reasons we gather is to remember: to remember who we are, whose we are, and what we are to be doing. One of the ways we do this work of remembrance is by our participation in the Lord's Supper, Eucharist, or Holy Communion. Like any human family, the family of God's memories are invariably tied to memories of family meals. This is as it should be. At the meal, around the Lord's Table, in the sharing of food and drink, in the invitation and initiation into that intimate and familylike table fellowship, in the table talk—the tales of family heroes, the stories, the tradition, the arguments, the teaching—we continually proclaim and enact who we are as the family of God. When we eat together as God's family, we remember. This chapter is about some of those shared memories of meals.[1]

Sunday Dinner

As I think back on my past, some of my earliest and fondest memories as a child are memories of family meals. Looking back, I realize that *our dinner table was a place of revelation, recognition, and identity.* It was around the dinner table, eating with members of my family and participating in the conversation there, that I learned what it meant to be a member of this family.

I particularly remember Sunday dinner. Sunday dinner was no minor meat-and-two-vegetables affair in our family. It took place at my grandfather's big, rambling house where we all gathered after church. "Family" meant more than one's father, mother, brothers,

45

and sisters. Family meant that entire army of cousins, aunts, uncles—including those passersby whose relation to the clan was less clear. The uncles gathered in the living room for cigars and arguments over cotton prices or the Sunday sermon. The aunts assembled in the kitchen for the preparation of dinner and arguments about whatever aunts argued about then. We children chased one another up and down my grandmother's big front porch or else played tag in the yard, oblivious to our parents' periodic pleas to be careful with our Sunday clothes and our cousins' skulls.

By two in the afternoon, uncles and cousins were starting to complain of famine, knowing full well that dinner would not commence for at least another hour. Someone made a periodic foray into the kitchen for a purloined biscuit. But mostly we waited in famished anticipation for the meal.

At last it came. We all gathered at the long dining room table, seated by the directives of my grandmother who always had firmly fixed in her mind exactly where everyone was to sit. One of the comforting things about life in those years was you had a place and you knew it: Mama at one end, Papa presiding over the ritual at the other end; aunts, uncles, and cousins fixed at their appointed stations in between.

The meal began with a seemingly interminable prayer by Papa. All having been blessed, the raucous, joyful falling upon the feast was begun, followed by a period of silence broken only by the tinkling of knives and forks. Then the table talk began. Cousins listened while aunts and uncles argued over the next county election, agreed that Republicans were ruining the country, and thoroughly discussed all matters of importance. When the elders spoke, all listened in attentive deference to the wisdom of the ages. Occasionally, some teenaged upstart of a cousin would offer an ill-considered opinion on the matter under discussion only to be hooted down by uncles and aunts or else patiently instructed in correct opinions by Papa or Mama. And there were stories: lots of stories about family exploits of the past, stories about heroes, funny stories, *our* stories.

Every Sunday, without variation, the ritual continued. We ate in an unbroken succession with all the forebears who had eaten at that table before us. As we grew older and had families of our own, more cousins for the clan, we took our places among the elders, moving up along the side of the dinner table, one seat closer to the chief elders of the tribe.

The point is nobody had to tell me what it meant to be a part of this family. Nobody had to tell me who I was or instruct me on the proper world view for folk in our clan. I never got instruction on orthodox belief or behavior. Nobody had to explain to me that I belonged and that I was loved. I learned all that at the Sunday dinner table. If you had asked me, "Who are your people and what do they stand for?" I would have responded, quite honestly, "My people are those who gather at Grandmother's dinner table." In later years I have come to see that table gathering as definitive of my family. Members of my family were initiated, nurtured, and claimed at the table. There we participated in the common family memory, fellowship, and identity. We found our place, our name, our story—at the table.

Meals and Memories

The ancient Jews understood. They also knew the table as a place for memory, fellowship, revelation, and identity. For the Jew, every meal is sacred, an occasion for remembering and enacting what it means to be a Jew. At the Passover meal, when the roast lamb is eaten, there is remembrance, story, and enactment that tell the participants at the table who they are. To this day, at the Passover seder (the order used at the Passover meal), when asked, "Why is this night special above all other nights?" the master of the seder proclaims to the folk around the table:

> We were Pharaoh's slaves in Egypt, and the Lord our God brought us forth from there with a mighty hand and an outstretched arm. And if the Holy One, blessed be he, had not brought our forefathers forth from Egypt, then we, our children, and our children's children would still be Pharaoh's slaves in Egypt.
>
> So, even though all of us were wise, all of us full of understanding, all of us elders, all of us knowing in the Torah, we should still be under the commandment to tell the story of the departure from Egypt. And the more one tells the story of the departure from Egypt, the more praiseworthy he is.[2]

The meal thus becomes an occasion for memories, memories of who they are as Jews, revelation of what it means to be a Jew. God's mighty act of deliverance in the Exodus is remembered not as a mere historical event but as a mighty act of redemption in which the persons at the meal are active participants. In eating this meal, they become part of that Exodus:

> In every generation let each man look on himself
> as if he came forth from Egypt.
> As it is said: "And thou shalt tell thy son in that
> day, saying: it is because of that which the Lord
> did for me when I came forth from Egypt."[3]

The Passover table, and its accompanying conversation, becomes an occasion for memory, recognition, disclosure, revelation, and identity. A Jew is not only one who is circumcised but also one who eats and, in the eating, remembers. In this Passover meal and its table talk, the Jews remember—not in the sense of remembering something in the past but in the sense of remembering who, by God's grace, they *are*.

Meals in Luke

Luke knew. When Luke recorded the life of Jesus, he recorded meals. Luke's Gospel depicts Jesus at a succession of meals, each of which reveals something important about who Jesus is and what membership in his kingdom means. Indeed, Luke–Acts reads like a newspaper society column; the Gospel's narrative seems to follow Jesus from one dinner party to the next. Luke believes that Jesus is best known by the company he keeps, particularly the company at the dinner table. At each of these dinnertime episodes significant things are revealed about Jesus and his kingdom through the company he keeps at table as well as the conversation around the table. At the table the participants of the kingdom are identified and Jesus reveals who he is and what membership in his kingdom means. The table is a place for revelation, recognition, and identity.

One of the chief criticisms of Jesus was not that he espoused unorthodox theology but that he showed bad taste in his choice of dinner companions. The Pharisees' charge that Jesus was a notorious "wine bibber" and one who "eats and drinks with sinners" (Luke 7:34) is rather well documented—particularly in the Gospel of Luke.

The first meal that Luke records is the meal in which Levi is the host (5:29-39). The meal at Levi's house sets the pattern for other meals in Luke–Acts. Note who is at table with Jesus: tax collectors (lackeys for the oppressive Roman government, bureaucrats who dealt in filthy, idolatrous lucre with Caesar's image on it) and other assorted sinners. A controversy breaks out because Jesus dares to "eat and drink with tax collectors and sinners" (v. 30). Jesus responds, "Those who are well have no need of a physician, but those who are sick" (v. 31). If one is well, one doesn't need a doctor! (The implication is that the sickest sickness of all is not to know how sick one really is!)

Then there is a controversy over the joy of the meal (vv. 33-39). The scribes and Pharisees say something like this: "The disciples of John the Baptist fast—we can tell they are religious—but *your* disciples eat, drink, and make merry." In other words, "We know the disciples of John the Baptist are religious; they look so miserable." And Jesus replies, "Can you make wedding guests fast while the bridegroom is with them? When the bridegroom arrives at a wedding, the guests eat, drink, and make merry. It is time for the party to begin." There is fresh new wine bubbling forth here (vv. 37-38), and it will bust old wineskins; a fresh, new joy will break forth that has been unknown in your deadened "religion."

Jesus and his disciples move from Levi's house to the wheatfields where, on the sabbath, they arouse the Pharisees' anger by plucking some grain and eating (6:1-5). This is unlawful. When objections are raised, Jesus challenges their dead religion of rules and regulations, reminding them of David's meal in the temple (vv. 3-4). The old laws give way to a new emphasis on human need and divine action to meet human need.

In the next major meal, a Pharisee is host (7:36-50). The Pharisees receive admittedly "bad press" in the Gospels, and Luke's Gospel is no exception. But remember that the Pharisees were the true "liberals" of Jesus' day, earnest lay persons who sought to relate their religion to every facet of their daily lives. Pharisaism was thus a noble attempt to allow the blessed law of God to permeate all of one's daily activity. In Luke, however, the Pharisees stand for religious self-righteousness and snobbery. Luke presents the Pharisee as, to use Mark Twain's phrase, "a good man in the very worst sense of the word."

Jesus is at the home of a Pharisee. Once again, an argument breaks out around the dinner table. When a weeping, penitent woman enters, wets Jesus' feet with her tears, wipes his feet with her hair, and then kisses and anoints them, it is more than the Pharisees are able to take. "If this man were a prophet, he would know who and what sort of woman this is who is touching him, for she is a sinner." In other words, "If this man were really religious, if he had prophetic insight, he would be able to tell what kind of woman this is." After all, what is religion for if not to enable one to discern between the good and the bad, the righteous and the unrighteous?

Luke goes to great lengths to show the scandalousness of Jesus' defiling contact with this sinner. Some scholars have suggested that the woman's "sin" was prostitution. We are never told explicitly what her notorious sin was, but the alabaster ointment, as well as her general behavior, when compared with stereotypes of prostitutes in that part of the world, indicate that she may have indeed been guilty of prostitution. Luke paints her actions toward Jesus in the most sensitive, sensual colors. And Jesus has allowed this woman to *touch* him. The Greek word for "touch" here is *hauptō,* which can mean, and may mean here, "to caress, to light a fire, to fondle." Obviously, a kind of scandalous eroticism permeates this encounter, which adds to the general scandalousness of the episode. Is this any way for a *real* prophet to be behaving?

Of course, the implication of the story is that both the Pharisee and the woman are sinners. One is a knowing, forgiven, grateful sinner; the other is an unknowing, pride-filled, self-righteous sinner—but they are *both* sinners. There are sinners who know they are sick and need a physician and there are sinners who do not know they are sick, but they are *both* sinners. And Jesus eats with them.

At a third dinner time episode in Luke, again the host is a Pharisee (11:37-52). This time the Pharisee is astonished that Jesus "did not first wash before dinner" (v. 38). The Pharisee's objection is, of course, based upon religious rather than hygienic considerations. Once again, Jesus is going against Scripture and tradition by not performing the prescribed rite of ceremonial washing before eating. Jesus calls the man a fool—a fool because he has gotten hung up on the externals of religion at the expense of the internals. Again, Jesus eats with sinners, albeit unknowing sinners whose sin is precisely that they don't know their sin.

These meals with the Pharisees culminate with a major sabbath meal at the house of a ruler (14:1-24). Here is a meal full of revealing table talk, parables, and parabolic gestures. Once again, Jesus shows that he is not a very compatible dinner guest! Once again, the host is a Pharisee. (Those Pharisees must have been gluttons for punishment—they keep inviting him back to dinner!)

A man who has dropsy is brought before Jesus. Jesus puts the lawyers at the table on the spot by asking, "Is it lawful to heal on the sabbath, or not?" They are silent (v. 4) because they realize that Jesus has just revealed the ludicrousness of their legalism. He heals the man, then asks them another parabolic question: "Which of you, having a son or an ox that has fallen into a well, will not immediately pull him out on a sabbath day?" (v. 5). Once again, they are silent. Their silence is revealing.

Then, noting how the guests at the feast are jockeying for prominent positions at the dinner table, he says, "When you are invited by any one to a marriage feast, do not sit down in a place of honor, lest the host invites a more eminent man than you to take your place" (see vv. 7-9). One ought to take the lowest seat, the dishonorable seat, so that when the host comes, he will say, "Friend, go up higher." He who humbles himself will be, in the end, exalted. What kind of behavior is this—the first will be last, the humble will be exalted, the lowly will be raised up?

Having finished off the guests, he now turns to the host (who has probably been enjoying Jesus' criticism of the pushy guests):

> When you give a dinner or a banquet, do not invite your friends or your brothers or your kinsmen or rich neighbors, lest they also invite you in return, and you be repaid. But when you give a feast, invite the poor, the maimed, the lame, the blind, and you will be blessed, because they cannot repay you (vv. 12b-14a).

Now what is this? This is a strange guest list for a feast. In that part of the world, in that day, where hunger was ever-present and a feast was a major event of days' duration, the thought of inviting these outsiders, these wretched ones, to dinner must have struck the host as strange indeed. Invite people whose only qualification for being invited is that they can never repay the invitation? What reward is there in that? Do you hear echoes, as this guest list is read, of Jesus' inaugural sermon in his hometown synagogue in Nazareth? (See chapter 6 where this sermon is discussed.)

> The Spirit of the Lord is upon me,
> because he has anointed me to preach good news to the poor.
> . . . to proclaim release to the captives
> and recovering of sight to the blind. . . .
>
> —4:18

When the disciples of John the Baptist came and asked Jesus if he was really the Messiah, Jesus replied: "Go and tell John what you have seen and heard: the blind receive their sight, the lame walk, lepers are cleansed, and the deaf hear, the dead are raised up, the poor have good news preached to them" (7:22). Here is a strange messianic kingdom indeed: a kingdom in which the outsiders become insiders, in which the wretched of the earth are royalty, in which the most poor—the least and the last—are the most prominent.

Overhearing all of this talk about banquets, one of the guests hears an obvious allusion to the great messianic banquet. What would the long-awaited Messiah do when he appeared? He would give a great banquet and invite Israel to come and be filled at the banquet table of the Lord. Isaiah foresaw that great feast as a time when the poor could come freely and eat and drink:

Ho, every one who thirsts,
come to the waters;
and he who has no money,
come, buy and eat!
Come, buy wine and milk
without money and without price.
—Isaiah 55:1

"Blessed is he who shall eat bread in the kingdom of God!" exclaims the guest (Luke 14:15). Oh, how happy we shall be when Messiah comes and spreads the great banquet for Israel!

"Do you wish to sit at that table?" Jesus seems to ask. "Here is what that table will look like." And Jesus tells them a parable, one of the most memorable in all the Gospels, the parable of the great banquet (Luke 14:16-24).

A man gives a great feast and invites all of his friends and cronies. He sends his servant to proclaim, "Come, for all is now ready" (v. 17). But the response of those who are invited is scandalous: They make excuses. One says he has bought a field and has not seen it. Another says that he has bought five yoke of oxen and must now examine them. Another has married a wife! By this time the hearers of the parable are probably rolling on the floor with raucous laughter. The excuses, especially when given in response to so great a feast, are utterly ridiculous. In that part of the world, where land and livestock are purchased at a premium, it would be unbelievable that one would buy such expensive items without first examining them. And what male of the ancient Near East would let a little thing like a wife keep him from attending a mighty feast?

The host is angered. In the Near East, to refuse an invitation to a man's table, especially for reasons so frivolous as these, is a great insult. The master sends the servant out again, this time to the streets and lanes of the city. Who are now asked to come in? "The poor and maimed and blind and lame" (v. 21). Does that guest list sound familiar? When Matthew tells this story (Matthew 22:1-10), he makes the point even stronger, saying that the servant gathered up "both *bad* and *good*" to fill the banquet hall (v. 9).

Switching from the singular to the plural "you," Jesus says to all, "For I tell *you,* none of those men who were invited shall taste my banquet" (Luke 14:2, italics added).

Can you feel the surprise, the shock of those who first heard this story? When the long-hoped-for Messiah appears and the banquet table is set, the response of the chosen, the first invited, is shocking—they stand outside, refusing to come in, refusing to accept the great invitation to the great banquet. The nice people, the healthy people, the chosen people make excuses, raise objections, quibble over the guest list, and, in so doing, end up on the outside. The outsiders, the last and the least, end up on the inside simply because they have nowhere else to turn but toward grace; they have nowhere else to go but to come and let their great hunger be filled by this great grace.

The Good News is that the empty are being invited to eat and be filled with good things. The poor, the sick, the sinful are coming into the kingdom first. Jesus' inaugural word in the Sermon on the Plain is being fulfilled: "Blessed are you that hunger now, for you shall be satisfied" (6:21).

Well, there we have some of the mealtimes and table talk with Jesus. The Pharisees' charge that Jesus is a glutton and wine bibber, one who befriends and eats and drinks with sinners, is undeniable. In so doing, Jesus demonstrates that he has come to free us from all bondage, even the bondage of our narrowly conceived religion. He has come to destroy all the barriers that we erect between "sinners" and "righteous." He sets himself at odds with tradition and with the religious establishment of his day. But he also reveals a new and revolutionary kingdom, a kingdom in which all the old values, the old standards of insiders and outsiders, right and wrong, sinners and righteous, are turned upside down and set in a new light. The presence of Jesus at each of these dinner time episodes sheds new light on the Gospel and foretells the promise of good things to come. Every major component of the Good News in Luke can be seen at every gathering at the table.

You will recall other meals in Luke: The party that was given to welcome home the prodigal son, in which the meal becomes a time of reconciliation and celebration (15:11-24), and the feeding of the five thousand in which the meal becomes an occasion to heal and nourish the hurting and hungry multitudes miraculously (9:10-17). These meals, too, become both revelation and enactment of the Good News.

The Last Meal

By far the most significant meal in Luke is that memorable meal in the upper room (22:14-38). Luke implies it was a Passover meal, an occasion when the people of Israel celebrated their memories and remembered who they were: redeemed, delivered, chosen people of

God. The Last Supper is depicted by Luke as an occasion for the disciples to remember who they are through their participation in the meal and through Jesus' teaching at the table. This is the only meal, of the ones we have mentioned, where Jesus is the host.

Jesus begins the meal by predicting, "I shall not eat . . . until it is fulfilled in the kingdom of God" (v. 16). In other words, he will not eat this Passover meal again until he eats the great banquet in the kingdom. He then takes and blesses the cup, predicting, "I shall not drink of the fruit of the vine until the kingdom of God comes" (v. 18). Then, as was the Jewish custom, after the cup is blessed the bread is blessed, broken, and given. "This is my body," Jesus says as he passes the bread around the table. The actions are the familiar table actions of any Jewish sabbath meal and are part of every Passover meal, even though the words accompanying the actions are unusual. This meal is significant not because the actions are unusual—they are not—nor even because the Words of Institution ("This is my body") are unusual. In the Middle Ages and in the liturgies of the Reformation, we focused upon those words at the exclusion of all other words in the meal. That was unfortunate. For the significance of this meal in the upper room is the same as the significance of all the other meals in Luke—in the table talk that occurs between Jesus and participants.

In his insightful analysis of the Last Supper, Paul Minear divides the table dialogue into four parts.[4]

First, Jesus drops the bombshell: ". . . behold the hand of him who betrays me is with me on the table" (v. 21). Note that *all* of the disciples are uncertain as to who will betray him, for "they began to question one another, which of them it was that would do this" (v. 23). Any at the table may betray him; no one is secure.

Second, there is a dispute among the disciples over which of them would be greatest in the kingdom (22:24-27). In the other Gospels, this argument occurs in other places (e.g., Mark 9:34). Luke, with a stroke of dramatic and theological genius, places it here. Here, at the very end of Jesus' ministry, the disciples show that they still have no understanding of who he is as the Suffering Servant and what his kingdom is as the kingdom of the poor and disinherited. All take part in the argument. The disciples—the twelve closest friends of Jesus who have heard his preaching, observed his ministry, who have been the recipients of his most intimate teaching—reveal, by this dispute over greatness, that they do not have the foggiest notion of what he has been talking about.

Jesus is among them not as triumphant Lord but as "the one who serves." He is the waiter, the deacon, the servant at the table. He now does, in serving them food and drink, only what he has done throughout his ministry with them—lovingly serve. Jesus waits on the table and goes to the cross to suffer and die as they argue about greatness. The disciples still think that following Jesus has something to do with greatness and reward. They have not heard his word about servanthood. They all reveal, in this argument, that they are still misunderstanding, ignorant, unfaithful, betraying followers.

And yet, it is to *these* ignorant, betraying, unfaithful ones that Jesus promises a seat of honor in the kingdom, promising them, "that you may eat and drink at my table in my kingdom, and sit on thrones judging the twelve tribes of Israel" (v. 30). *These* are the ones with whom he chooses to share food and drink—his twelve best friends—even if they happen to be his twelve betraying friends. Jesus not only eats with them, betraying sinners though they may be, but he also *serves* them. *He* serves *them.* As in the footwashing scene when John tells this story (John 13), Jesus enacts before them the loving service that they are to practice in the world.

Third, Jesus focuses upon Simon Peter (Luke 22:31-33). "Satan has demanded to have you" (the "you" here is plural), Jesus tells Peter (v. 31). The plural "you" suggests that Satan has entered all the disciples, that no one is safe from the tempter's snare, that all will be tempted to deny him. But Jesus prays for Peter in the midst of his temptation, interceding for the disciples in their time of trial. Even in the midst of his disappointment at the disciples' misunderstanding and betrayal, Jesus prays for them that they may be strengthened.

Finally, the table talk climaxes in a strange conversation about swords (vv. 35-38). This has always been a problematic dialogue. Why would Jesus tell his disciples to get ready to use their swords (which seems an incongruous thing for him to say in the first place) and then, when poor Peter tries to use his sword against the Romans (vv. 49ff.), harshly rebuke Peter? It all seems very strange.

Some have suggested that this talk about being prepared with purses, bags, and swords is the risen Christ saying to the early Christian community to be prepared to live within the difficulties of the end time. But Paul Minear offers a more intriguing conclusion. Why, Minear asks, when Jesus has practiced nonviolence through his ministry, would he now change? What is happening here? Minear suggests this possibility: Jesus reminds the disciples that, when he had sent them out in ministry, he told them to take nothing with them along the way. In putting complete trust in him, they lacked nothing (v.

35). Then he asks them, in effect, "Do you have swords with you now?" In other words, "Did you obey me when I told you to take nothing, or have you taken along a sword just in case my power proved lacking?" Two swords are brought forth immediately, two swords that testify that the disciples disobeyed Jesus' earlier command not to trust purses or swords. Minear speculates that the two swords may be related to the two witnesses that are required, under Deuteronomic law, to convict a person of a capital crime. In other words, Jesus says, "Are there two witnesses to the crime of your disobedience?" The "two witnesses" are presented. Jesus says, perhaps sorrowfully, "It is enough" (v. 38).

And so they go out to the Mount of Olives where Jesus prays and urges the disciples to "pray that [they] may not enter into temptation" (vv. 40, 46). But they sleep. And when the soldiers and captors come to seize him, both the disciples and the captors have swords. They *both* participate in powers of darkness. There is no difference between the action of the disciples and the actions of the captors. "No more of this!" commands Jesus as he is led away to die while the disciples flee.

It's a sad, dark story, full of ignorance, fear, and betrayal. And yet it's also a joyful story. For behind the events of this fateful meal lies the same Good News that underscores the other meals that Jesus ate with sinners. Even in the midst of his disciples' sin, Jesus promises these betrayers a place at the new banquet table to come (vv. 28-30). He goes to prepare a place for *them.*

He eats, at this last supper, with virtually the same kind of dinner companions with whom he has shared his other meals—sinners— even if *these* sinners happen to be his twelve best friends. And it is these sinners who are the recipients of his service, his prayers, his promises, his love.

Remember, please, that this "Last Supper" is not, as the story turned out, the last of the meals with Jesus. This is not the last chapter of the story but rather the beginning of the story. For on that Sunday, on the first day of the week, as two despondent disciples walk dejectedly down the road to Emmaus, a stranger appears and walks with them (24:13-35).

The stranger asks, "What are you talking about as you walk?"

Sadly they respond, "Are you the only one in Jerusalem who doesn't know what happened?"

The stranger says he does not know; so they tell him about how they had hoped that Jesus of Nazareth would be "the one to redeem Israel" but that he had been put to death (v. 21). The disciples are so blinded by their despair, their faith is so shattered by the events of the past week, that they fail to recognize the risen Christ. They are blind to the mighty work that is occurring before their very eyes. "And beginning with Moses and all the prophets, he interpreted to them in all the scriptures the things concerning himself" (v. 27).

When they arrive at Emmaus, the disciples bid the stranger to stay with them. "When he was at table with them, he took the bread and blessed, and broke it, and gave it to them. And their eyes were opened and they recognized him. . ." (vv. 30-31). How interesting that it is not until *he is at table with them* that their eyes are opened. They do not even see him when he interprets the Scriptures (v. 27). It is only in those familiar servant actions of taking, blessing, breaking, and giving of bread that they are given revelation and recognition. It is only at the table that the Scripture makes sense, that their eyes are opened, and that they at last begin to understand. And the disciples run all the way back to Jerusalem to tell the others "what had happened on the road, and how he was *known to them in the breaking of the bread"* (v. 35, italics added).

The disciples then wait, as the Christ instructs them, in Jerusalem "until you are clothed with power from on high" (v. 49). That promised power is not long in coming. "When the day of Pentecost had come, they were all together in one place. And suddenly a sound came from heaven like the rush of a mighty wind. . ." (Acts 2:1-2).

The promised Spirit descends and strange things happen. For Luke, one of the most surprising things that happens is that all these diverse and disparate peoples—those Parthians, Medes, Elamites, and all the rest—sit down and eat together. The story of Pentecost, the birthday of the church, climaxes with Luke's assertion that "they devoted themselves to the apostles' teaching and fellowship, to the breaking of bread and the prayers" (v. 42).

Perhaps it is not too far afield to say that the real miracle of Pentecost was not that the Spirit descended making sons and daughters prophesy, young men see visions, and old men dream dreams (v. 17); the miracle of Pentecost was that these diverse races and nationalities were so joined together in Christ that they were enabled, by the Spirit, to break bread together and partake of food "with glad and generous hearts" (v. 46).

Had not Jesus promised his disciples, before his crucifixion, "You may eat and drink at my table in my kingdom" (Luke 22:30)? After Pentecost, in the early church's eating and drinking together, the church experienced the beginning of that new age, a foretaste of that promised messianic banquet. It felt the presence of the risen Christ in its midst in its Sunday celebrations of the Lord's Supper. "Christ our Passover, is sacrificed for us," Paul could say, "therefore let us keep the feast" (1 Corinthians 5:7, author's translation).

In eating together, the church remembered the many memorable meals that Jesus shared with his disciples. The church remembered, as it ate and drank, that Jesus never ate with anyone but *sinners*—harlots, Pharisees, scribes, tax collectors, disciples. Some were knowing sinners and some were unknowing sinners—all were equally loved, taught, nourished, and served by Jesus at the table.

The Invitation

Sometimes in my travels I encounter a congregation where, when the Lord's Supper is celebrated, many people in the congregation refrain from receiving Communion because they think they are "unworthy." Some misguided, if well-meaning, person has probably misinterpreted Paul's warning to the Corinthians (1 Corinthians 11: 27-29) so that some of the congregation is now fearful to receive the bread and wine "in an unworthy manner."

I can think of nothing more sad than to hear the invitation given and yet see someone standing outside, refusing or fearful to join the feast. I want to tell these hungry people who stand outside, whether they stay away because they think that they are too good or whether they think they are too bad: "Remember, the Gospels say that Jesus ate only with sinners, only unworthy *sinners*." Every time the church gathers to celebrate the Lord's Supper, it remembers and discovers, to its never-ending surprise, that the risen Christ continues to choose the same dinner companions today! Thank God.

I'm glad Judas was there, as well as Peter, and the harlot, and the Pharisees. Because, if they had not been there at the table with Jesus, I would not be able to be here with Jesus at the table today.

Who is Christ's church? That gathering of sometimes faithless and sometimes faithful hungry disciples who gather to break bread in Jesus' name and are thereby fed. What is the purpose of the church? To be gathered and fed by Christ and invite all humanity to his great gospel feast. It is as simple and mundane and yet as mysterious and profound as that. It is nothing more, nor less, than a meal.

5

Baptism: Death by Water

ROMANS 6:2-11

Gentile or Jew
O you who turn the wheel and look to windward,
Consider Phlebas, who was once handsome and tall as you.[1]

Whenever I am asked, "What does the church believe about baptism?" I always respond, "The church believes everything about baptism which we all believe about water." While knowing about water is not all one needs to know about baptism, it is the right place to begin. Baptism first means everything that water means.

But when I then ask, "What does water mean?" I invariably receive answers like "cleansing," "refreshment," "life," "birth." All of these images are both true to our own experience of water and are also New Testament ways of speaking about baptism. But even these rich images of water do not say enough. They overlook a predominant New Testament way of speaking about baptism and the primary way in which Paul speaks about baptism—baptism is death.[2]

The Baptism of Jesus

Water is not only the source, origin, and sustainer of life; it is also a potential terminator of life. Our bodies may contain several gallons of water; but a teaspoon or so in the wrong place will bring instant, suffocating, terrifying death. The human fetus develops gills before lungs, but the human being is also born with a deep, primordial fear of death by drowning. We moderns tend to romanticize water. We focus upon its cleansing properties—its natural, fresh, and refreshing uses. But old Israel knew better. For the children of Abraham water was a thing to be dreaded—the surging, dark, bubbling chaos of nothingness and death. In the beginning when God began creating, one of the first necessary acts was to tame the waters. Heaven, a "firmament," was needed to separate "the waters above from the waters below" (Genesis 1:6-8). The waters below were then contained, driven back, gathered together so that "dry land might appear" (v. 9). And this was good.

In the other creation story of Genesis 2 a river gives life to Eden, and water is acknowledged as the source of life—an unavoidable fact of life in the dry Near East. But a few chapters later, water is also acknowledged as the source of death and destruction, an equally unavoidable fact in the frequently and often devastatingly flooded Near East. Noah goes into the ark and watches as the death waters rise, forever rise, during those dark, wet forty days and forty nights while God "blotted out every living thing that was upon the face of the ground . . ." (7:23).

But upon those same waters of death Noah, his family, and the creatures were preserved until there was once again dry land upon which to stand. Life began again as death waters receded and a rainbow testified to a new covenant. Never again need the earth fear annihilation by water.

But water continued to be a primal and primary biblical image for death and destruction. Thus, the psalmist, describing himself "sunk in misery," cries out.

> Deep calls to deep
>   at the thunder of thy cataracts;
> all thy waves and thy billows
>   have gone over me.
>   —Psalm 42:7

Let other nations put their ships to sea and sing of the glories of the ocean. As for Israel, she preferred dry ground, the solid and sure footing of the Promised *Land*

And so it is with more than casual interest that we watch as Jesus appears on the banks of the Jordan and asks to be plunged into the water by John. The story of John the Baptizer is told with remarkable similarity by all the Gospels. John is depicted in the tradition of the Old Testament prophets as a prophetic preparer of the way. He is a pre-Christian figure who points the way to the One who is to come. The preparation that John urges is a preparation of a "baptism of repentance." People are to repent and be baptized, to get ready, to be washed and clean for the coming of the Messiah. John's baptism is presented as a preparatory, temporary stage in God's dealings with his world: "I have baptized you with water, but he will baptize you with fire," John predicts.

The church might rightly ask, "Why was Jesus baptized by John? What did Jesus need to prepare for or repent of?" Past Christians sometimes worried over the questions of the sinfulness or lack of sinfulness of Christ, which are raised by his baptism. We do not need to trouble ourselves with these past arguments except to say that Jesus seems to affirm John's baptism on its own terms (Mark 11:30), that is, as relating to sin and repentance.

But it is also clear that Jesus' baptism is something much more than mere repentance. When Jesus is baptized by John, John's baptism is transformed from a sign of human preparedness to an occasion for divine activity. The heavens open, the Spirit descends, a claim is made. The baptism of Jesus is a sign that there is now nothing more to await or prepare for: God is present in Christ. It is therefore not so much a ritual of preparation but a ritual of inauguration. The kingdom of God is present, in the midst of us, in the presence of the One who is shown through this baptism to be God's Son in whom he is well pleased.

But in what way is Jesus the near presence of God? His baptism is the revelation not only of Jesus' identity as the awaited Messiah but also of the unexpected nature of his messiahship. This Messiah comes not (as some were expecting) as a military overlord but rather as a servant. He is the obedient one, "fulfilling all righteousness," more than he is the ruling one. In his baptism is revealed what was to become the pattern of his entire ministry. In this sense, John's baptism of repentance from sin is related to John's baptism of Jesus. In being baptized by John, Jesus thus identifies himself in solidarity with the sinners whom he has come to save. He shows forth the surprising lordship of the Lord who is servant to those whom he has come to save.

And what is the nature and content of that service that this Savior comes to render? Jesus' baptism is also revelation of that. On two different occasions Jesus himself is depicted as using the word "baptism" to refer to his own impending *death*. He asks his wayward disciples, "Are you able to drink the cup that I drink, or to be baptized with the baptism with which I am baptized?" (Mark 10:38). And as he moves steadily toward the cross, Jesus says, "I have a baptism to be baptized with; and how I am constrained until it is accomplished!"

(Luke 12:50). Jesus himself forges the link between his baptism and his death. His death on the cross is his submission, his obedience even unto death, his "baptism." Jesus thus shows, as he submits to John's baptism in the Jordan, the radical way in which he will confront the sin that enslaves humanity, meeting it on its own turf, submitting even to death in order to save through his servanthood, a servanthood even unto death.

John's baptism, while not erased by Christ, is given much deeper meaning as Christ himself submits to baptism. In Christ the repentance, the *metanoia,* the "turning around" that John called for is intensified, even to the point of death. John may have presented his baptism as the washing away of sins, but Jesus seeks a more radical confrontation with sin than a cleansing bath. He seeks nothing less than death. In the baptism of Christ the new and intensified chapter in the story of God's dealings with his people is initiated. In this New Age, a servant is sent who is God himself, in his flesh, who will meet and defeat evil in its own territory, as a life-and-death encounter.

This may account for the fact that we have little record that Jesus or his disciples baptized anyone during his earthly ministry. Jesus' proclamation was not a simple call to repentance in the sense that John preached repentance. Rather, Jesus' own baptism was the beginning of a ministry of obedience that would not be fulfilled until he was obedient even unto the cross. Baptism was the beginning of his death, the first visible adumbration of the radical quality of his servanthood. Jesus and his disciples did not baptize because it was not yet time. The full dealings of God with the world had not yet been accomplished; Jesus' own "baptism" had not been fulfilled.

It was at the cross and the tomb that his "baptism" was finally accomplished. There his saving work, begun and shown forth at his own baptism in the Jordan, was done. The last enemy had been met and defeated. God's love for the world was fully revealed. The depth and seriousness of human sin, the subtlety and power of evil as well as the depth and power of God's love, met and were revealed upon the cross. "It is accomplished," Jesus victoriously and obediently pronounced from the cross as he died.

Now the saving work having been done, the "baptismal" process having been completed, Jesus commands his disciples to begin their saving work, entrusting them with the inauguration of his reign in the world: "Go therefore and make disciples of all nations, baptizing them in the name of the Father and of the Son and of the Holy Spirit. . . ." (Matthew 28:19). The *disciples* are now to go out and "make disciples." How are disciples made? Disciples are made by "baptism" and "teaching" (see vv. 19-20). In Acts, after the "pouring out of the Spirit" and the birthday of the church (Acts 2), at the end of Peter's Pentecost sermon to the wondering crowd, the crowd asks, "What must we do to be saved?" Peter's response is simple: "Repent, and be baptized every one of you in the name of Jesus Christ for the forgiveness of your sins; and you shall receive the gift of the Holy Spirit" (Acts 2:38-39). Baptism is the passageway into discipleship, the fitting response to the proclamation of the gospel.

The Womb and the Tomb

But even if Christ were baptized, even if his baptism signified his servanthood unto death and his obedient solidarity with sinful humanity unto death, why, then, would his disciples understand themselves as commanded to continue the practice of baptism? In what way is baptism seen as initiation into the kingdom of God and the passageway to discipleship?

There is no better place to seek out the early church's understanding of baptism than in the writings of Paul. For Paul, baptism is many things—adoption, birth, cleansing, circumcision, light. But above all, baptism is *death.* In coming forth for baptism, in "submitting" as Jesus submitted to John, the believer shows that he or she is truly "in Christ," that is, that he or she is in the same death-rising process as Christ. Paul reminds those Colossians who continue to dabble in "elemental spirits" and human "philosophies" that such prebaptismal paganism will not do. "You were circumcised," he tells them. Like the children of the Old Israel, you were initiated into a new status, a new way of living. What is this "circumcision of Christ"? It is baptism:

> You were buried with him in baptism, in which you were also raised with him through faith in the working of God, who raised him from the dead. And you, who were dead . . . , God made alive together with him. . . . He disarmed the principalities and powers and made a public example of them, triumphing over them in him (Colossians 2:12-15).

In baptism the Christian is yoked to the death-rising Christ event. Behind every Christian baptism is this "baptism" of Christ.

"Remember who you now are," Paul tells the wayward Galatians. "It is now too late for your old values and prejudices. You are all children of God." Paul reminds them: For as many of you as were baptized into Christ have put on Christ. There is neither Jew nor Greek, there is neither slave nor free, there is neither male nor female; for you are all one in Christ Jesus (Galatians 3:26-28). Baptism is not only the washing away of the previous distinctions and boundaries of the old age, but also it is the very death of such sinful distinctions. Baptism not only expresses the death of the old ways and old points of view, but it also actually brings about that death. As Paul told the Colossians, "For you have died, and your life is hid with Christ in God" (Colossians 3:3).

In other words, Paul sees baptism as summing up everything that Christ means to the world. No clearer statement of this summary can be found than in his letter to the Romans. In chapter 5 of that letter Paul eloquently testifies to the free, unmerited grace of God in Christ. But in chapter 6 he qualifies his statement on grace by speaking to those who may misinterpret what this free grace means for the Christian. Some may say, "If grace is so free, why not sin all the more so that God can spread around more grace?"

For Paul, the person who asks such a question has forgotten the meaning of his or her own baptism:

> . . . How can we who died to sin still live in it? Do you not know that all of us who have been baptized into Christ Jesus were baptized into his death? We were buried therefore with him by baptism into death, so that as Christ was raised from the dead by the glory of the Father, we too might walk in newness of life.
>
> For if we have been united with him in a death like his, we shall certainly be united with him in a resurrection like his . . . our old self was crucified with him so that the sinful body might be destroyed, and we might no longer be enslaved to sin. For he who has died is freed from sin. . . . So you also must consider yourselves dead to sin and alive to God in Christ Jesus (Romans 6:2-11).

Being baptized "into Christ" is a reenactment of what happened to Christ. The result of such death is "newness of life." It is *God* who is the active agent of this baptismal work. While we are the passive recipients of the burying, the uniting, and the enlivening work of God in baptism, God's work with us has continuing, radical, moral implications for us. The fruits of baptism are essentially a changed life "in Christ." The one who is baptized is a "new creation" in which the old sinful body and its old servitude no longer hold us. We are dead to that old self and "alive to Christ."

These ethical implications of baptism are typical of Pauline baptismal thought and clearly separate Paul's views of Christian baptism from some of the essentially self-centered, self-gratifying purification washings of the water rites among the Hellenistic mystery cults of Paul's day. Christian baptism is not merely a repeatable washing of someone so that he or she can be clean enough to achieve personal immortality. Christian baptism is nothing less than *death* and nothing more than the creation of a new being who lives by a radically different system of values of obedience, servanthood, and community. Behind every baptism is the "baptism" of Jesus, his death and resurrection, which opened up the new age. Paul simply drew out more clearly the relationship between Jesus' baptism and death and our baptism "into Christ" as well as the ethical implications of this relationship.

Whenever Paul speaks about the work of Christ in us, he seems not to know whether to speak in terms of "birth" or "death"—baptism "into Christ" felt like being killed and being born at the same time.

Volunteering for Death

The early church fathers continued to be impressed by the death-life feel of the Christian baptismal experience. In fourth-century Jerusalem, Cyril, in his post-baptismal catechesis, explains to the newly baptized:

> Then you were led to the holy pool of divine baptism, as Christ taken down from the cross was laid in the tomb already prepared. Each one was questioned. . . . You made the profession of salvation and three times were you plunged in the water and came forth, signifying Christ's burial for three days. By this action, you died and you were born, and for you the saving water was at once a grave and the womb of a mother.[3]

In the Western church, Ambrose also explained baptism as death:

> Whoever is baptized, is baptized in the death of Christ. What does this mean: "in the death"? That, as Christ died, you also must taste death: as Christ died to sin and lives for God, so you also must die to the past pleasures of sin by the sacrament of Baptism, and rise again by the grace of Christ. . . . When you plunge into the water, you receive the likeness of death and burial. You receive the sacrament of His cross. . . . And you, when you are crucified, you are joined to Christ, you are joined to the gift of Our Lord Jesus Christ.[4]

A favorite baptismal figure of the fathers was Noah. In the Deluge they saw a prefigurement of the destruction and deliverance that baptism effected. The Red Sea was also frequently mentioned in their writings, a symbol of destruction and freedom. As Paul had said, ". . .our fathers were all under the cloud, and all passed through the sea, and all were baptized in Moses in the cloud and in the sea. . . ." (1 Corinthians 10:2-5). Baptism was usually done during the Easter vigil, at least until the early Middle Ages. Baptism during the Christian Pasch not only provided a further linkage of our "death" in baptism with Christ's Passion and death but also beautifully symbolized the baptizand's "passover" from slavery to freedom, from death to life, from darkness to light in baptism.

The Reformers were also much impressed with the death-life theme of baptism. While Reformation liturgies continued the Augustinian stress upon baptism as a washing away of sin (which had become overstressed in medieval baptismal liturgies to the point of obscuring other meanings of baptism), both Luther and Calvin often referred to the baptismal experience as death. Continuing, even accentuating, the late medieval penitential emphasis (which was probably another overemphasis) upon human sin and guilt and the need for divine forgiveness, the Reformers were equally concerned with the need for continuing human *response,* the necessity for the response of faith and righteous living while taking care not to detract in any way from the efficacy of divinely given baptismal grace.

In his *Small Catechism,* Luther asks, "What does baptism mean for daily living?" His answer: "It means that our old sinful self, with all its evil deeds and desires, should be drowned through daily repentance, and that day after day a new self should arise to live with God in righteousness and purity forever." In baptism the "old Adam" is drowned. But, as Luther observed elsewhere, "the old Adam is a mighty good swimmer." The Protestant Reformers, to a man, were convinced that our sin is so complex and deep-rooted a phenomenon in our thinking and willing that only a thousand conversions and a lifetime of repentings would root it out. Conversion and repentance are continuing baptismal work.

When we repent, we merely ask the God who has buried us in baptism to continue his work of putting us to death. We volunteer for death. We turn to God, like little children, and say, "I can't save myself. You must do it for me." "I can't be good. Make me good." "I can't preserve my life. Take my life and hide it in your love." This is repentance talk that is also baptismal talk. This is why repentance is constantly spoken of by the Reformers as a return to baptism. We never get too old, or too pure, or too righteous to be exempt from the need to die to our old selves and rise to Christ.

Our conversion is therefore a continuing living out of the death-life experience of our baptism, asking God to do for us what we can never do for ourselves, to finish the saving work in us which was begun at our baptism. Baptism is a once-and-for-all sacrament that takes one's whole life to finish. Conversion is part of the baptismal process with a final goal that is no less than the total refashioning of our sinful, disobedient, proud selves into more what God intended for us. It is birth that only comes through death. You do not get that kind of radical transformation in a moment. It takes a lifetime of death and resurrection to make so radical a change.

The old baptismal prayers in the *Book of Common Prayer* said:

> O merciful God, grant that the old Adam in these children may be so buried, that the new man may be raised up in them. Amen.
>
> Grant that all carnal affections may die in them, and that all things belonging to the Spirit may live and grow in them. Amen.
>
> Grant that they may have power and strength to have victory, and to triumph against the devil, the world, and the flesh. Amen.

How different is the understanding of the Christian life in these prayers from that which is held in some circles of American evangelicalism where the gospel is offered as the solution for human problems, the fulfillment of human expectations, and a good way to make nice people even nicer. Baptism, as revealed in these ancient prayers, is often the beginning of problems, the destruction of our expectations for human self-fulfillment, the ultimate challenge to our delusions of goodness. "When we were right," said Luther, "God laughed at us in our rightness." Baptism says that our problem is not that we have a few minor moral adjustments that need to be made in us so that we can be good; our problem is that we are so utterly enslaved to "the devil, the world, and the flesh" that nothing less than a full-scale, lifelong conversion will do. Nothing less than daily, sometimes painful, often frightening death will do. As my colleague at Duke, David Steinmetz, has put it:

> Every conversion has a price. Something is gained, but something is lost as well and the loss may prove to be painful. . . . The gospel not only resolves problems which trouble us; it creates problems which we never had before and which we would gladly avoid.[5]

Wrath and judgment of God are poured upon us along with God's acceptance and love. He may take me "just as I am without one plea," but he will not let me be until he has finished what he has begun in my baptism. Sometimes God's work in me is very painful. But God destroys our old decadent selves, buries our past, sweeps through our prejudices, inundates our self-centeredness not simply to destroy;

death comes in order that a new reality, a new being may take its place. The death is for the sake of life, and that dying and rising are a daily affair.

From Death to Life

The newest doors of Saint Peter's in Rome are the great bronze doors of the contemporary Italian sculptor Giacomo Manzu, the artist friend of Pope John XXIII. On one door is depicted a series of death scenes: "Death by Falling," "Death in War," and others. To some it may seem strange to welcome people into this great church with images of death upon the front door. But we must. We must speak of death first, in the same way as the church often placed its baptismal fonts just inside the front door of the church. This reminds us that to be baptized, to enter the church, is to volunteer for death—again, and again, and again.

The striking Argentinian evangelical, Juan Carlos Ortiz, when he baptizes someone often uses this baptismal formula: "I kill you in the name of the Father, and of the Son, and of the Holy Spirit, and I make you born into the Kingdom of God to serve Him and to please Him."[6]

Sometimes I wonder if in most of our celebrations of baptism we reduce the waters of baptism to a mere sprinkle, covering them up with sentimental rosebuds and lace because we dare not speak about that strange work that is starting to happen on this day. You know how we always try to avoid death with euphemistic cover-ups.

While washing is perhaps the most obvious of all meanings of baptism, we must never forget that what happens in baptism and its continuing consequences is much more drastic than mere washing. As soon as the church started thinking (contrary to the New Testament) of baptism as chiefly cleansing, it started thinking in terms of cleansing from *past* sins; it started nagging people to keep themselves clean. This only leads to the eternal frustration of those who know they can never stay pure enough for God or to the eternal delusion of those who think they are.

Baptism is nothing less than the death and burial that lead to new life. "For you have died," Paul says, speaking in the past tense; "and your life is hid with Christ in God" (Colossians 3:3), he says, speaking in the present and future tenses. We live as dead persons who have lost hope in the world and in their own pride, but we also live as those who know they have been raised from death in order that they may be claimed as God's own. We are the subjects of a divine work that is more drastic, more revolutionary, more painful, more promising, more far-reaching than mere washing. "Become what you are! Die that you might live!" is stronger talk than the mere "Be clean."

To be baptized is to be condemned to die. It is dress rehearsal for the last day as well as for every day in which we must die to all that would make us less than God wants for us. Baptism is also resurrection practice. Between our death in baptism and our next death, we live in the hope that the same God who raised us from the waters of baptism will raise us up again, pulling us forth from the tomb like newborn babes from the womb. We live in the confidence that comes from baptism because we have already been through a trial run of our death and resurrection. We do not fear what we have already done.

Pity the poor new Christian at baptism! This person may not know it, but he or she has only begun to die!

But in that death—life.

6

Preaching:
Serving the Word

LUKE 4:16-30

While prayer, the Lord's Supper, and baptism are central acts of worship, for most Protestants preaching continues to be the central worship activity—for some, alas, the *only* meaningful liturgical activity. As we noted in chapter 1 the New Testament contains examples of early preaching. But how does the Bible preach? Not "How do we preach about the Bible?" but "How does the *Bible* preach?"

I contend that there are, within the New Testament, models for interpretation and proclamation of Scripture. The Bible is always in dialogue with itself and the church of its day. By observing the dynamics of that dialogue, contemporary preachers can receive guidance in their present dialogue with Scripture in sermons. This chapter moves from a contemporary sermon to a sermon that preacher Jesus delivered, then back to the contemporary sermon in order to discover what the New Testament tells us about biblical preaching.

The Merely Moral

I have just returned from being preached at in Duke University Chapel. I say "preached at" because that is mostly what happened. I feel as if I have been to a modern version of a medieval flagellants convention. The old flagellants got their backs beaten bloody in hopes of exorcising the plague. They felt that only a sound thrashing could make things better. I have just been whipped with words: nagged, berated, and then urged to "go out and liberate the world from oppression." Frankly, I am in a rather oppressed state myself.

In a way, Duke Chapel is a fitting place for such penance. It is a magnificent neo-Gothic monument, built by a Methodist tobacco tycoon, standing in neo-medieval grandeur under a hot sun in the guilt-filled South. A tradition whose founders once rebelled from old Mother Church and her petty penance in order to reassert the primacy of God and God's grace returns home to its medieval roots, settling itself down again in the predictable equations of moralistic religion.

The preacher for the day no doubt finished his sermon quietly congratulating himself for his "prophetic" pronouncements. I gathered that he considers himself somewhat of an activist. While he would probably consider it a great compliment to his preaching if some member of today's congregation were to react angrily to his sermon by yelling at him and walking out, I expect that about all his sermon received was a polite academic yawn. The students, faculty, and visitors who were in Duke Chapel today have already heard the sermon, or ones just like it, a dozen times over.

As I walked from the chapel after the service, I was reminded of a remark that has been attributed to Paul Scherer: "There are four kinds of American religion which can and must die: the merely therapeutic, the merely intellectual, the merely emotional, and the merely moral." It is the "merely moral" that concerns me now, because preaching that is little more than moralistic platitudes—whether it be the "Six Ways to Live a Better Life" variety or "Three Reasons Why You Should Boycott Lettuce" brand—is reducing our preaching to something that is both petty and inconsequential. Such preaching is another example of how we often let ourselves get in the way of God in our worship.

Text or Pretext?

It is self-evident to most of us, particularly those of us in the Protestant tradition, that our preaching ought to relate to Scripture. The Christian preacher is the bearer of the Word, the "servant of the Word," as H. H. Farmer once said. The Christian community entrusts to its preachers the task of interpreting and proclaiming the Scripture, the verbal tradition that we hold to be the fullness of revelation and that continues to hold us in its power. This is the unique burden that the preacher bears, the unique service that he or she renders to the church. While the average congregation probably wants help for daily living, ethical instruction, clarification of doctrine and inspiration from its preacher, surely it is fair to say that it expects these wants to be placed within the context of the Christian community, its tradition, and its Book. People expect a unique confrontation with the Word when they hear sermons, and it is the preacher to whom is entrusted the task of hearing and speaking God's truth in the midst of God's people at this time and in this place.

But while we may all affirm that the Scriptures play a vital role for the believing community, it is not always clear exactly how they function in the preaching of the church. In an attempt to help clarify how the Scriptures are employed in preaching, I would like to return to today's preacher and his text, comparing how he used the text with the way Jesus himself used the same text in a sermon of his own.

The text for the day was Jesus' sermon in his hometown synagogue in Nazareth (Luke 4:16-30), which Luke places at the beginning of Jesus' ministry. During a regular sabbath service Jesus is invited to read and interpret the Scriptures. He reads from Isaiah (61:1-2), impressing people with his reading ability. Then, as was the custom, he sits down to interpret the Scripture that he has just read. Here is where the trouble starts. Jesus' sermon so enrages the people that they rise up and attempt to kill him—as strong a negative reaction as any young preacher could fear to receive!

The chapel preacher took this episode in Nazareth as his text on this third Sunday after Epiphany, choosing to focus mainly upon Jesus' quote from Isaiah:

> The Spirit of the Lord is upon me,
> because he has anointed me to preach good news to the poor.
> He has sent me to proclaim release to the captives
> and recovering of sight to the blind,
> to set at liberty those who are oppressed,
> to proclaim the acceptable year of the Lord.

This the preacher interpreted as a call from Jesus himself addressed to us. After directing a few barbs at the neo-charismatic movement for "perverting what the Spirit really is," he then asserted that the Spirit is "that which motivates us to be about the work that God wants us to do." And what is that work? You guessed it. We are to "preach good news to the poor" (which "does not mean actually to preach to them but to work for justice for all poor people—that would be good news to them"), to "proclaim release to the captives" ("How many people right here in North Carolina are political prisoners, and what have we done to help them?") "and recovering of sight to the blind" ("How many people among us are blind to the real needs of our fellow human beings?"), "to set at liberty those who are oppressed" ("Many times we are more on the side of the oppressors than on the side of those who suffer oppression"), and "to proclaim the acceptable year of the Lord" ("*Now* is the time for you to decide whose side you are on and to get busy with the Lord's liberating work!").

The sermon ended with an appeal to "get serious about following where the Spirit is leading us today." We all stood and sang what was called a Hymn of Dedication—"God of Grace and God of Power"—and then we went home.

Was this a biblical sermon?

Preacher Jesus

If Jesus had repudiated Scripture as source and guide for the revelation of God to God's people, we would have no hermeneutical problem. We would simply need to "follow the Spirit," or read today's newspaper, or listen to where people say they are hurting, or heed some other contemporary source of revelation. But Jesus did *not* repudiate Scripture. He cited Scripture, taught from it, and debated his foes on the meaning of its testimony. (Mark 2:23-28 and 7:1-14 are examples.) On the basis of this evidence we can inquire into Jesus' own principles of interpretation, particularly in regard to how the Old Testament Scriptures functioned in the early church. This can be done as a way of seeking clues for our own use of Scripture in preaching.

Luke places Jesus' sermon at Nazareth in the opening scene of the public ministry. Since there are indications that Luke's placement of the story is chronologically wrong, we can assume that there may be some theological motive for Luke's departure from the Marcan outline. It is probably set here, at the beginning, as Luke's early theological answer to the troublesome question of why Jesus was rejected and crucified. It therefore provides a preview, a foreshadowing of the entire mission of Jesus. Why did Jesus' own hometown kith and kin, the good folk at Nazareth, reject him? What turned them from admirers, when he had finished reading the Scriptures, to an angry homicidal mob when he interpreted the Scriptures? What was there in his worship leadership and preaching that first attracted them and then repulsed them? There was something about the way Jesus interpreted the tradition, the Scripture, which enraged them. It was his preaching that made his cross inevitable.

The worship at Nazareth that day began predictably enough. Luke sets the scene as one that occurred in a predictable, customary, and thoroughly commonplace way on a sabbath day in Nazareth. Jesus is at the place of his roots, "where he had been brought up," in the synagogue "as his custom was" (Luke 4:16). He reads a popular passage from Isaiah, a passage widely interpreted as a foretelling of how the long-awaited *eschaton* would take place: A herald will come, God's anointed one, who will proclaim the "acceptable year of the Lord" for the poor, the captives, the blind, and the oppressed.

The Dead Sea Scrolls have shown that this passage was prominent in the preaching of first-century Palestine. Various apocalyptic, ascetic groups like the Essenes lived by this text, practicing a life of poverty and self-abasement, assuming that this prophesied coming of God's anointed one would be a blessing for them and judgment upon the "unrighteous." James Sanders supposes that the good synagogue-going folk at Nazareth likewise assumed that this passage foretold good things for them.[1] After all, were not they oppressed by Rome? Were not they the wretched of the earth, the poor? Who would be more deserving of good news, release, and liberty than *they*?

When Jesus reads this text on this sabbath, a certain sense of satisfaction settles upon the folk of Nazareth: the satisfaction of knowing that whenever the "acceptable year" comes, it will be *their* year for their blessing and their deliverance. And when the young preacher then proclaims, after the text is read, that *"today this passage is fulfilled,"* a shock of excitement runs through the congregation. *This* is the day. *Now* is the time for reckoning and reward. *We* will be free at last. *We* will at last be the recipients of that which we have so long expected.

But then one of the hearers asks, "Isn't this the carpenter's son?" (v. 22). (In Mark's parallel story [Mark 6:1-6] he is called "Mary's boy.") Perhaps, like the Essenes, the folk at Nazareth are expecting that the "Lord's anointed" will be a heavenly figure, someone able to put out the Romans and restore Israel to her good fortunes, somebody to come give them what they deserve, what they expect—not Joe and Mary's boy.

In answer Jesus quotes an old proverb: "No prophet is *acceptable* in his own country" (v. 24, italics added). What did he mean? Sanders points out that all of the Old Testament prophets were local boys. They all spoke to their own people. But all the judgmental Old Testament prophets were rejected. They proved to be unacceptable. Why? Because, says Sanders, any preacher who takes the familiar, comfortable words of our tradition and interprets them in such a way as to challenge the very people who find their identity and take their comfort in that tradition is a preacher who will often receive unacceptance as response to his or her preaching. Jesus reminds the people of old Elijah and Elisha (vv. 25-28), who were unacceptable because of their behavior toward the outsiders over in Sidon and Syria. Was this any way to treat the insiders in Israel? "No," said the people of this older prophet's day. They were unacceptable. The anointed herald is "to proclaim the acceptable year of the *Lord*." Jesus, like the prophets before him, is not acceptable simply because a true prophet proclaims what is acceptable to *God*—not what the people want to hear. The true prophet is more intent on interpreting the nature and workings of God than on fulfilling the needs and wishes of the people.

Like us, the folk at Nazareth assumed that what is acceptable to us is acceptable to God. After all, does it make good sense to be faithful if God does not somehow honor our faithfulness? Is it not reasonable to assume that those of us who preserve and honor the Scriptures will reap the benefits of the fulfillment of the Scriptures? It is disconcerting to us and to the folk at Nazareth for some young preacher to speak about the latecomers into the vineyard receiving as much pay as those of us who have sweated it out all day (Matthew 20:1-16). It is unpleasant to hear about one who looks down the road and sees the waiting father run to embrace somebody else (Luke 15:11-32) or to hear of those who read other persons' names on the place cards at the great banquet table (Luke 14:15-24). This is, to say the least, most unacceptable. It is enough to make us want to throw such a preacher over a cliff or something (Luke 4:29).

Note in this Nazareth sermon how a given text of Scripture is used in conjunction with texts from other parts of the Scripture. Jesus interprets the Isaiah tradition by reminding the people of two biblical stories of Elijah and Elisha. He thus interprets Scripture through Scripture. This rabbinic hermeneutical practice of bringing together two originally separate texts is called *midrash.* Scripture is thereby put in dialogue with other Scriptures in order to achieve a mutual interpretation, an enriching juxtaposition that results in a meaning that was lacking in the "plain sense" of either original statement but now opens up new levels of meaning for the contemporary community of faith. In this way a familiar text, such as the Isaiah passage, is given new bite by being interpreted through the juxtaposition of two other texts whose authority was admitted. Jesus' interpretation presupposes that the meaning of the words of Scripture is not exhausted by their original context but that the Scripture remains a living vehicle of present revelation of God.

While some earlier biblical critics tended to dismiss such instances of *midrash* as vestiges of questionable rabbinic interpretation that were created and interpolated into the Jesus story by the church, recent commentators have suggested that passages such as Luke 4:16-30 may be well-preserved examples not only of Jesus' parabolic teaching but also of Jesus' scriptural interpretation. Rather than dismiss such traditions, we can use them to discover how the Scriptures functioned in the preaching of Jesus and the early church.

The folk at Nazareth are offended by Jesus' sermon because he turns the tables on them; he entices them into the Scripture, then flips the Scripture back upon them through the juxtaposition of other Scripture. Jesus, in his interpretation of the Isaiah text, reminds them:

> But in truth, I tell you, there were many widows in Israel in the days of Elijah . . . , when there came a great famine over all the land; and Elijah was sent to none of them but only to Zarephath in the land of Sidon, to a woman who was a widow. And there were many lepers in Israel in the time of the prophet Elisha; and none of them was cleansed, but only Naaman the Syrian (vv. 25-27).

Elijah was the eschatological figure who was expected to return and "proclaim the acceptable year of the Lord." But Jesus reminds the people that it was the historical Elijah who angered Israel when he challenged the people's narrow views of God by going over to Sidon and spreading God's grace. And it was old Elisha who chose an outsider like Naaman to heal, in spite of all the other good sick people who were insiders. And these reminders strike all of the insiders at Nazareth as blasphemy against Israel and her expectations. It surely is blasphemy to say that, in the end, the coming Lord will not embrace only Israel. It is enough to make a congregation want to put such a preacher away.

But the same corruption of perception infects us even as it infected the folk at Nazareth. Why are we not as offended by Jesus' sermon as they were? Where is the surprise, the contemporary bite in the text for us? There is no offense here for us because we have heard Jesus in the same way as the people of that day heard Isaiah. We assume that Jesus in this sermon is proclaiming his rejection of Jews and his acceptance of Gentiles. But to interpret the passage this way, as some biblical scholars do, is to destroy the prophetic bite of the text and to ignore what the Gospel itself reports to be Jesus' own homiletical interpretation of Old Testament Scripture.

The Bite and the Burden of the Text

To recover the bite and the intention of Jesus' sermon is to restore not only the prophetic intention of this passage in Luke but also to rediscover the way in which Scripture functions in the preaching of Jesus. To recover this, we must ask ourselves why it was so maddening that day to have Jesus read Isaiah and then remind the congregation of Elijah and Elisha. Our own distorted perceptions lead us to believe that we have progressed to the point of finding Jesus' words in this sermon, or any other, to be predictable, sensible, acceptable. We assume that we do not get angry because we are now enlightened to the point of agreement—not like the angry folk at Nazareth that day.

Every generation assumes that yesterday's prophetic word made yesterday's believers angry. But we—the enlightened, educated, *really* faithful ones—we hear the prophets gladly.

> Woe to you, scribes and Pharisees, hypocrites! for you build the tombs of the prophets and adorn the monuments of the righteous, saying, "If we had lived in the days of our fathers, we would not have taken part with them in shedding the blood of the prophets." Thus you witness against yourselves, that you are sons of those who murdered the prophets (Matthew 23:29-31).

Our self-righteousness reveals that we contemporary sons and daughters of those who stoned the prophets share the same corruption of perception that led our mothers and fathers to welcome Elijah, Elisha, and Jesus with brickbats.

As the preacher in Duke Chapel said, we believe that we in the church have a responsibility to help the poor, the outcast, the oppressed of the world. Jesus is so right that we should be doing these good things. This is thoroughly *acceptable.*

But the problem with the text is that *that is not what Jesus preached on that day in Nazareth.* What Jesus said that day, and said with consistency throughout the Gospels, was that Israel (the church for us) lives under the judgments and scrutiny of God. Israel is called to bear the burden of the truth of God, a truth which transcends Israel's (the church's) narrow boundaries and puny notions of God.

One of the problems with our interpretation of this text, or nearly any other, is our proprietary interest in God. We assume that *we* are the proprietors of God's grace; we are the society of the elect, the sole possessors of God's love. God's grace is no longer gift to us because it is so utterly expected. It is our right, our privilege, our achievement.

This is the blasphemy against which the prophets spoke. The prophet Jesus took the older prophets' passages and preached them in an unexpected way by telling people that the prophet of the end-time, Elijah, would come and do what the Scripture in Kings (1 Kings 17:1, 8-16) said the prophet Elijah did originally; that is, he would go outside the "elect." It is difficult enough to convince ourselves that our own benevolence must be shown to the outsiders, but then to be told that our God is *their* God, too—this is maddening. Like the folk at Nazareth, we, too, start to wonder what good is our faithfulness, our honoring of the Scriptures, our good deeds for the poor, outcast, and oppressed if God is going to go out and love so promiscuously? If there is not something we can believe to be right or if there is not something we can do to act right, then who can be assured of righteousness? If this is the way God plays the game, how can we be assured of our victory?

It is the church that bears the burden of the truth of God; the church is the servant of God's truth, the body that forever stands under the judgment and blessing of that truth. And it is the church that is, therefore, forever in danger of housebreaking that truth. In so doing, we end up with no more burden to bear than that of the rest of the world's tamed, agreeable, acceptable truths. We end up with nothing more to say to the world than that which it can hear hawked on any street corner.

Jesus' sermon reveals our own corrupted perception of the tradition. Our God is not our privileged possession, not the agreeable housepet for the church, not the one who gives us pleasant errands to run in order that we might be rewarded for our good deeds in his behalf. Our God is the One who is over all, beyond all, in all, for all. The Scripture can be heard again only when we stop identifying ourselves with Jesus (because, contrary to the preacher's interpretation of the text in Duke Chapel, it is the *Lord* who comes to do these things for humanity, not *us*) and start seeing our faces among that congregational mob at Nazareth. Everything hinges on where you find yourself in the text. In this way we again feel the burden of the text, the bite of its truth, and thereby be judged and redeemed from our normally corrupted perception. To stand constantly under the burden of that truth, to serve only the Word and its words, allowing ourselves to be judged by the very message we bear, is our mission.

Theocentric Preaching

Jesus, in his own preaching as revealed in Luke 4, begins theocentrically. The starting point in his preaching is not some moralistic human requirement for what we are to do, but the revelation of what *God* is doing. His radically theocentric interpretation does raise questions about human conduct. In another incident in Luke 18:18-30, a rich young man asks, "What must I do to inherit eternal life?" When his disciples hear Jesus' response to the man's question, they wonder, "Then who can be saved?" Jesus, in turn, answers them with an affirmation of what *God* can do to bring even rich people through the needle's eye into the kingdom. Matthew (19:16-17) knows that the real cause of the disciples' bewilderment is their difficulty in sorting out their desire for some assurance of doing good from the truth that there is only "One . . . who is good." Jesus' word is primarily about God and secondarily about human response.

In Nazareth, and elsewhere, Jesus' preaching and his interpretation of the Scriptures concern themselves with *God's* identity and activity in the present. True, because of this revelation, human response is called forth, but only as *response* to the primary revelation. The Scriptures speak of God. Our response is never prior to the revelation of who God is for us. Matters of human response must never be the primary starting point for our dialogue with the Scriptures.

This is the interpretive principle that I think can be derived from the preaching and interpretation of Jesus himself. It is only after we are addressed by God that we are challenged to respond in a way that can be faithful to God. Our identity and activity can only be surmised after the revelation of God's identity and activity for us. If God's self-revelation to us in the Scriptures were immediate and simply analogous, then our interpretation of Scripture would require no care and study. But such is not the case. We do not immediately know how we resemble the folk at Nazareth until we know who they were and who God was for them. Then we can better proclaim who God is for us. We must know who God is before we can know who we are. We must discern what God is doing before we can decide what we are to do. Indicative precedes imperative.

If the question of the rich young man, "What must *I do?*" is the beginning of our search into the Scriptures, our inquiry is immediately limited to what we deem to be possible, permissible, acceptable human behavior. We argue over whether God would dare require us to do this or that. We seek no grace from God because we have no need of it in our busy working out of our own salvation. The focus is upon what we are to do rather than upon what God may be revealing to us about what he is doing for us. We end up with all sorts of petty directives for human conduct, or the labeling of social or political programs as divinely ordained, or at worst, trivially nagging.

American preaching, in Duke Chapel and nearly everywhere else, has taken an anthropocentric starting point for its scriptural interpretation. Homiletical moralism attempts to isolate a text and establish a one-to-one correspondence between the circumstances of places like Nazareth and those of places like North Carolina. The resulting message is put forth as the will of God for us, the way to get ourselves right with God and thus be assured of God's election. This way, we do not need God. The old hellfire-and-brimstone revivalists worked on the smoking-drinking-cursing sins; new "prophetic" social activists work on the racism-sexism-nationalism sins.

The sins may be different, but somehow the underlying sin manages to stay the same—putting our good deeds in place of God, *starting with ourselves rather than God,* depending upon our ability to keep our slates clean rather than upon God's grace. Such preaching certainly has no need of Jesus dying upon a cross and rising from the dead to make itself acceptable to an American pragmatic, self-help, self-saved society; particularly at places like Duke where the academic establishment offers a myriad of ideologies and techniques for auto-salvation.

In place of this anthropocentric starting point for our scriptural interpretation and preaching, I think Jesus' own preaching suggests a hermeneutical model that starts with God. The avoidance of moralism or the laying down of general principles for behavior may not yield instant behavioral results. But we must remember, in our preaching, that we are seeking God rather than "results." We are wondering what God is doing before we ask what we should do. God is the "hero" of these stories—not Israel, not the church, not the preacher, not you, not me.

When John Wesley found himself, to his great surprise and even embarrassment, standing out in an open field and preaching to the Kingswood coal miners, he chose to preach this text to these wretched men:

> The Spirit of the Lord is upon me,
> because he has anointed me to preach good news to the poor.
> He has sent me to proclaim release to the captives . . . ,
> to set at liberty those who are oppressed,
> to proclaim the acceptable year of the Lord.

The rough miners heard him gladly. But later, when he preached the same text to a more established congregation in the sophisticated Church of England, he was sent packing and told never to preach there again.

"Nothing is more repugnant to the religious sensibilities of educated people than to be told that justification comes from God alone," Wesley told a friend in a letter that he wrote shortly after his eviction.

And it still is.

Looking for God

Specifically, what form might this theocentric style of interpretation take? For one thing, while it would use the tools of scientific, historical-critical investigation of Scripture, it would deny that such investigation is equivalent to the theocentric task of "serving the Word." We are required to use the wide range of modern critical skills that are available to us in order to uncover the historical encounter of God's people with God's revelatory Word, at the same time reminding ourselves that we, too, are historically conditioned even in our present criticism of the Scriptures. We must see ourselves in the same kind of historically conditioned bind as the folk at Nazareth. We must admit to the same expectation—to be told that we must go out and fix the world on *our* terms just as the folk at Nazareth expected to be told that God's anointed One was coming to fix the world on *their* terms. Careful criticism helps put some of the prophetic bite back into the tradition by recovering the past situation of the text as well as the situation of the present interpreters of the text.

At the same time, "serving the Word" means that one stands under the Word as a member of the covenant community; that community bears a burden of proclamation that is greater than mere historical exegesis. We stand under all the Scriptures, both testaments, which dynamically inform and critique one another *as they are informing and criticizing us. "Scriptura Scripturae interpres"* was the way the ancient church said it; texts within the church's canon are to be read in mutual interdependence as God's Word for us in our time and place, much the same way as Jesus preached at Nazareth. This is more dynamic than purely historical recovery. The end result of our exegetical work is not just to uncover the original message of the text but to uncover and to feel the weight of what the Scriptures are saying to us in our time and place.[2]

The difference between some of our current applications of the historical-critical method and the older "serving of the Word" is that in sermons like Jesus' sermon at Nazareth, the text is not merely interpreted by the community, but it also interprets the community. This self-critical method arises from the hermeneutical principle that *we* are historically conditioned, not just the biblical texts. The context for our interpretation, the audience for the message of the text, is the believing community and its Scripture, a community that studies and interprets Scripture solely to serve the Word; to bear, be judged, criticized, convicted, and thereby saved by the Word. We do not exegete a given passage of Scripture as an interesting piece of historical detective work; we study the text because it is *our* text, a word from God for *us*, and we will not leave it until we feel its full prophetic weight upon *our* shoulders.

Service of the Word only has meaning within the context of the community's life and worship. Outside that context we can have no meaningful encounter with Scripture, nor will we be significantly encountered by Scripture. It is in worship that we gather to bear together the burden of revelation and then to make our response to that revelation. It is for this worship task that the preacher studies the Scriptures and prepares sermons—not the proclamation of doctrine, or codes of behavior, or emotional fervor, or programs for social advancement—but rather the proclamation of God's identity and activity in the present. The preacher is bound in service to the Word as one who shares the historical and cultural condition of the community, whose weaknesses and corrupted perceptions are not unlike those of others within the community. The preacher's face is in the *congregation.*

While it is also the preacher's task to summon the community to respond, in worship and in the world, to the Word, the preacher's first task is to "open up the Scriptures" (see Luke 24:32) to seek the Lord who is revealed therein. Then the preacher is to help the community respond in concrete ways to that Lord. But the preacher's struggle to help people formulate a proper response must never come before the prior task of serving the Word through the study and proclamation of the Scriptures. It is the identity of God that is to be sought first—our identity and our response arise out of that seeking and finding.

The Service of the Word

I left Duke Chapel today not much different than when I came. I was not blessed, enraged, warmed, motivated, judged, or graced by the sermon—not because the preacher did not strive very hard to do all of this to me! In fact, I expect that I—*my* blessing, *my* rage, *my* warmth, *my* motivation, *my* judgment, and *my* grace—was uppermost in the preacher's thoughts throughout his preparation and delivery of today's sermon. And that was the problem.

Someday I might tell that preacher not to worry so much about me. I am not the one he is called to serve. My thoughts, my action or inaction, my morals, my acceptance or lack of it is not the proper focus of his vocation as preacher. Nobody has anointed this preacher to give good or bad news to me, to release, to recover, or to set me at liberty. The only thing we in the church ask of that preacher is to serve up the Word, to bear the burden of the text—unacceptable or acceptable though it may be for us. It is God whom we are expecting in this encounter with our Scriptures—God. Those of us in the pew are not as in need of protection from God as the preacher may think. We are, most of the time, willing to be brought face to face with God, prepared to be proved wrong and to stand naked and judged in order that we might be recreated and made new. In the presence of the Word we might not know what we are to do, or what step to take next, or what we are asked to think or affirm or confess. But we are willing to bear the unknowing if only we can be assured that the One whom we are struggling to know is none other than our life and our light. Serve us that Word, and the preacher will have served us indeed.

7

Worship:
The Healing Vision

MATTHEW 17:1-9

No doubt you think it strange in our exploration of New Testament worship to be asking again, "Why worship?" But now, having spoken specifically of Scripture reading, prayer, the Lord's Supper, baptism, and preaching, let us again speak more generally, as we spoke in chapter 2, of the purpose of all our worship.

Why do you come to church on Sunday morning? "I come for a moment of peace, to get away from my problems," says one person. Another disagreed. "I come to church only to get motivated to live a better life in the real world."

In the first person's view, Sunday morning is a time to escape the problems and pain of the "real" world. In the second view, Sunday worship is a time to get the energy or insight to go back to the "real" world where the action of faith really is. Both views assume that the "real" world is somewhere other than in the world of worship.

Escape? Avoidance? Why are we in worship on Sunday morning and what should we legitimately expect from that worship? To answer those questions, I take you to a key biblical story about worship, the story of the Transfiguration (Matthew 17:1-9), once again setting my (and I hope, *our*) story within the context of the biblical story in order to let biblical worship inform our worship.

Worship and Work

My seminary days were in the late sixties. In many ways it was a difficult, dark time. The Vietnam war raged on over there while, over here, cities burned. Drugs and violence plagued the campuses.

Chants of "Hell no, we won't go!" blended with "Burn, baby, burn!" in a cacophonous litany of chaos and disorder. For the students of my seminary generation, work in the library was secondary to work in the streets. Social activism thrust us out of quiet sanctuaries—religious or academic sanctuaries—and into the clamor of the streets.

The worst of times was also the best of times. The Age of Aquarius sang and danced in idealistic, youthful exuberance and assured the troubled world that "all we need is love." Students may have been misguided and hopelessly naive in political matters, but they were concerned and involved. We cared, even if we knew not how to show we cared. We wanted a faith that made sense in the streets, face to face with the concrete needs of others, rather than the hothouse, aloof faith of the temple. There were many aspects of our youthful revolt against the old order which were less than admirable. In retrospect, however, we really don't look all that bad, particularly when compared with the academic and theological narcissism I have seen in many of the seminarians of the seventies and the beginning eighties.

Looking back, from the perspective of one who has now passed that dreaded over-thirty age mark of which we were so suspicious, I think our greatest flaw was that we had too little an appreciation for how tough things are for those who really try to live out their faith in the world. *Time* magazine called us the "Now Generation." We thought that we could have justice, liberation, equality, and peace *now.* All we needed, we assumed, was to get the right person in the White House, a slightly more enlightened foreign policy, a larger portion of the budget for the war on poverty, and all our work would be done.

Our "inadequate anthropology," to put it in a theologian's terms, led us into a gross underestimation of human sinfulness and an equally gross overestimation of our power to change others and ourselves. Evil, corporate and individual evil, proved more persistent than we thought. Our efforts to remove Lyndon Johnson from the White House ensured the election of Richard Nixon. Old, simple problems like racial segregation gave way to new, complex problems like busing, nuclear energy, and unjust distribution of wealth.

As the sixties ended, fewer people came to the mass demonstrations and marches. They drifted off the streets and into the more private concerns of self-fulfillment, self-discovery, and self-enhancement. Tom Wolfe's "Now Generation" of the sixties became the "Me Generation" of the seventies and the "Purple Generation" of the eighties.* I do not think we gave up because we no longer cared. I think we gave up mostly because we no longer had the emotional or spiritual energy to act. We were just plain tired.

I had been warned that this would happen. A friend of mine, a minister in a black church, foretold that it would not take long for the concern and activism of us white liberals to run out of steam. He remembered the early days of the civil rights movement in Mississippi. Busloads of high-minded, sensitive activists arrived from the North to help in the struggle for freedom in Mississippi. They came to lay themselves on the line, to "join hands with our black brothers and sisters." They came to march, to risk imprisonment and even death, if necessary.

But what was the first thing Martin Luther King and his cohorts did? They gathered everyone in some hot, crowded, little black Baptist church and sang and prayed and sang some more. "Well, this was all fine, if you like that sort of thing," thought the good, white, humanistic liberals. But what in the world did this interminable preaching and praying and singing and shouting have to do with the real business of gaining the rights of black people? My friend said that many of the white visitors wondered aloud, "Why are we here in the sanctuary when we should be out in the streets?"

In fact, many of the visitors probably wondered if archaic behavior, such as all this praying and singing, contributed to the problems of black people. "Opiate of the masses," was how somebody once described it. Many of those good, white liberals who sat there, fanning their dripping faces and listening to the fifteenth verse of "I've Been Washed in the Blood," probably caught themselves longing for a time when black people would finally be liberated from these quaint vestiges of their past so they could get on more quickly to the *real* business of political action.

"You see," said my friend, "we black folk had been at this thing longer than you white people. We knew that two hundred years of evil wouldn't be eradicated in one march to Jackson. That preachin' and those prayers and songs kept us going for all those years, and they would be the only thing that would keep us going. Without the power of God, without the vision of God, we wouldn't last long out in the battle."

---

*This term was used by Tom Wolfe in an appearance on the *Today* show. He explained it as applying to the eighties as a generation of style, where style and glamor are more important than substance.

Without the worship, there would not be any work. In all that perfectly "useless" singing, praying, and preaching, black folk were getting the strength to carry on, to march, to act, to move:

> Precious Lord, take my hand,
> Lead me on, help me stand. . . .

They withdrew for worship so that they might return with renewed perseverance and vision.

Is that why, once the way got long and hard, once the cameras focused elsewhere, once the sun came up and the road got hot, once a few laws were passed and the easy goals gave way to more difficult ones, most of us got back on the bus and headed for home? It was not that we no longer cared. We were just tired. Our eager, beneficient, secular, humanitarian impulses just gave out.

The Vision on the Mountain

In the second Sunday of Lent, as the church makes its weary way toward the cross on Good Friday, the Gospel lection is Matthew 17:1-9—the story of the Transfiguration. The story speaks of withdrawal and return—a dynamic that is found throughout the Gospels. I take Matthew 17:1-9 to be a statement about the inner dynamic of withdrawal and return which is at the heart of Christian worship and is therefore at the heart of the Christian life.

But the story is difficult to understand. It is certainly difficult to understand how it happened. It is no less difficult to know *why* it happened. Perhaps most difficult of all is to know what the story has to do with us.

The Transfiguration is described as a "vision" (Greek, *horama*). Though described in ordinary words, it is still strange to us. But it is not so strange in the context of the many biblical visions. Jesus leads his disciples up to a "high mountain" (compare Ezekiel 40:2; Matthew 4:8; 28:16), which everybody from Moses on knows is the best place to receive a vision. The shining face is standard for visions (Exodus 34:29-35; Revelation 1:16), as are the white garments (Luke 24:4; Acts 1:10), the cloud (Exodus 13:21-22; 16:10; Ezekiel 1:4; 10:3-4; Acts 1:9), and the divine voice (Exodus 24:16; Numbers 7:89; Revelation 10:4, 8).

Furthermore, Peter, James, and John all react to this strange vision characteristically; they fall on their faces, filled with awe (Numbers 22:31; Ezekiel 1:28; 43:3; Daniel 8:17; Revelation 1:17). What we have here is a classic theophany with the classic biblical reaction—fear, awe, dread. In other words, what we have here is a classic experience of worship—somebody is coming face to face with God.

I note that worship then involved a different reaction than is elicited today in worship. When is the last time you were *afraid* on Sunday morning? Our current backslapping conviviality and chumminess with God would seem strange to those who once stammered and shook before the divine, falling flat on their faces before God rather than shouting out a hearty "Good morning!" But that's another sermon.

When the Transfiguration is critically picked apart, a few interesting details come to light.[1] Jesus is "transfigured" (Greek: *metemorphōthē*). His appearance is changed; his clothing shines—similar expressions occur sixteen times in Revelation to denote heavenly beings or heavenly things. Moses and Elijah—one the lawgiver, the other the great prophet—were both commonly thought to be messianic heralds. Their reappearance would signify the arrival of the Messiah.

Upon seeing Moses and Elijah, Peter blurts out, "Lord, it is well for us to be here!" and then offers to make three tents or booths for each of the figures. Peter thus wishes to extend the stay of Moses and Elijah, thinking the messianic age has come. Moses and Elijah will dwell permanently with them, when "the dwelling of God is with men" (Revelation 21:3-4). But it is not yet time. The heralds of the age have been seen, but they have not come. The Messiah is present, but he has not yet begun to rule.

Then comes the cloud, a sign of the presence of God, as it had been in the Exodus. From the cloud a voice speaks, "This is my beloved Son, with whom I am well pleased," echoing that baptismal voice heard when Jesus began his ministry (Matthew 3:17). As at his baptism, for a moment the veil of the present is stripped away to reveal who Jesus is and who he will be. The disciples are now told not only who Jesus is but also that they are to "listen to him."

The revelation fills the disciples with awe. They fall prostrate until Jesus comes and touches them, saying, "Rise; do not be afraid." Matthew had closely followed Mark up to this point in the story. Up to this point, Matthew has mainly edited out Mark's redundancies. The major Matthean additions are verses 6 and 7 of chapter 17: the fear of the disciples and Jesus' quieting of their fear by his reassuring touch and the words "fear not." These conscious additions by Matthew are of crucial importance in understanding this story as Matthew's church understood it. Simply put: On the way to the cross, the disciples are given a dazzling vision of who Jesus is, more explicitly, who Jesus is in relation to the two great Jewish heroes, Moses and Elijah. The vision strikes fear in the hearts of the disciples. But Jesus touches them and tells them to "rise, fear not."

But what does the strange story mean? What does it mean for *us*? Most sermons that I have heard on this text tend to read the story closer to the way in which Luke tells it, noting that the disciples are led by Jesus from the mountaintop vision to the human pain down in the valley. The disciples long to stay upon the mountain, but Jesus leads them back down to the valley where they encounter the pitiful father bringing his epileptic son to be healed (vv. 14-20). The point of this interpretation is that Jesus demands his disciples to unite the divine glory of the mountaintop experience with the human suffering of the valley. This is a beautiful thought, and a valid one for Christians. But is this the point of Matthew's story?

There are problems with this interpretation. Unlike Luke, Matthew has five verses of intervening materials which discuss Elijah as well as Jesus' coming suffering (17:9-13). His concern here is with the suffering of Jesus rather than humanity's suffering. This breaks the flow of the narrative from the mountain to the valley. While many interpreters make a great deal of Peter's wish to build three booths or tabernacles and thereby remain indefinitely on the mountain of vision, this interpretation is also questionable. The "booths" that are suggested by Peter are not for Peter, James, and John to live in. Besides, the dialogue about building the booths does not appear to be the natural climax or major point of this powerful story.

The other favorite interpretation is to fix upon the phrase, "Jesus only," saying that the vision means that the Old Testament figures of Elijah and Moses depart, leaving Jesus only, thus pointing to the superseding of the Law and the Prophets by Jesus. This is an interesting point. However, it is a point that comes into some conflict with Matthew's other material concerning Jesus' place within the Law and the Prophets. ("Think not that I have come to abolish the law and the prophets; I have not come to abolish them but to fulfil them" [5:17].) We have the feeling that this is not the major thrust of the story, the major burden of the text. We wonder if the key to interpreting this story, particularly as Matthew told it, is to focus upon the concluding climax of the story, those verses that Matthew has added to Mark's (or somebody's) older account: "When the disciples heard this, they fell on their faces, and were filled with awe [fear]. But Jesus came and touched them, saying, 'Rise and have no fear' " (vv. 6-7).

This is the concluding command and word of Jesus. This is the proper climax to Matthew's story and the way in which the vision ends.

On the Way to the Cross

The celebration of the Transfiguration as an event in the church's worship was a relative latecomer to our liturgical year. Easter, Pentecost, and Christmas are older festivals. The Transfiguration arrived in the Western church's liturgical calendar, by way of the Eastern church, during the fifteenth century. August 6 was the date for the festival, during the season of the Trinity. However, Anglican lectionaries, reading the Transfiguration as an Epiphany story, place the festival on the second day after Epiphany. Lutheran lectionaries have traditionally placed the Transfiguration on the last Sunday after Epiphany, just before Lent. The new lectionary of the Roman church, as well as the ecumenical lectionary of many Protestant churches, now places the Transfiguration on the second Sunday in Lent. When interpreting a text, let us never forget that the Bible is the church's book. The church wrote it to be used within the church's worship. The Bible makes "sense" only within the context of the church and the church's worship. The worshiping, praying, believing, praising, searching community of faith is the starting point for all hermeneutics (interpretation). Therefore, let us set this passage within the context of worship and see what we learn.

Liturgically, the Transfiguration can be fruitfully understood from any one of the church's seasonal perspectives: Trinity, Epiphany, or Lent. The story makes sense in the context of the celebration of the Trinity. It is a Trinity story in that it reveals something about the nature of the three-in-one Godhead and its relationship to the church. Viewed as a revelation about the nature of the Christ, Peter's suggestion—that three booths be built, "one for you and one for Moses and one for Elijah"—is wrong if Peter, as the early church, means to recognize three equal sources of divine authority: Moses, the Law; Elijah, the Prophets; and the teachings of Jesus. A voice from heaven declares, "This is my beloved Son, with whom I am well pleased; listen to him." The authority of Jesus, the "beloved Son," is greater than the Law or the Prophets. The Law and the Prophets are not abolished in Jesus (Matthew 5:17); they are fulfilled, brought to fruition through his teaching. Ebionism is heretical because it assumes the old covenant is equal or superior to the new. A naive biblicism, which puts all Scripture on the same level, will not do either. While Jesus' teaching in Matthew in no way negates the Law and the

Prophets, everything he has said in his five great Matthean discourses stands under the shadow of the word: "This is my *Son* ; listen to *him.*"

The story also makes sense in the context of the celebration of the Epiphany. It is an epiphany in that it reveals, in one shining and stirring moment, something of profound significance about God. Epiphany is the season of the magi, who see that the Babe is also the King of kings; John the Baptist, who sees that the poor carpenter's son is the Lamb of God. The Transfiguration is *the* epiphany of all epiphanies. Before the eyes of ordinary disciples Jesus is transfigured. They see. His glory is made manifest. The riddle is solved. In this moment of worship, in the dazzling, mystical moment of revelation, the commonplace is opened up into epiphany and we *know,* we can *see,* with burning brightness, who he is.

But the story (and I think this is the insight of some of the new lectionaries) is also a story that properly belongs in the season of Lent. Consider the context. The first stage of Jesus' ministry, at least as Matthew presents it, is over (4:17–16:12). Jesus has preached his Sermon on the Mount, the apostles have been given their mission, and a series of parables and teachings about the kingdom have been given. Then comes Peter's confession, "You are the Messiah, the Son of the living God" (16:17). Here, at the point of Peter's confession, a second stage begins, a stage which Peter and the other disciples cannot accept (16:22-23) but which is part of Jesus' special brand of lordship: "From that time Jesus began to show his disciples that he must go to Jerusalem and suffer many things from the elders and chief priests and scribes, and be killed, and on the third day be raised" (v. 21). The second stage is the way toward the cross. The cross casts its shadow over every word and deed after this point—including the Transfiguration.

This is why the Transfiguration, as an experience of divine worship, is best understood as a Lenten experience. It happens on the way to the cross. The pace quickens; the end of the drama comes into view over the horizon; the actors act their parts in the tragedy, a tragedy that will end in death for Jesus and the scattering and disillusionment of his disciples. And, on the way, there comes this mountaintop experience that looks toward the cross and yet transfigures the cross by its burst of light before the encircling gloom.

It is that foreboding shadow, the shadow of the cross, that makes this story shine all the brighter. But it is not the light but the shadow that the disciples find incomprehensible. "God forbid, Lord! This shall never happen to you" (v. 22). Surely this is not how the kingdom comes! Nevertheless, Jesus continues to predict the cross for himself and for his followers (v. 24). Discipleship eventually leads to the cross. In the midst of these forebodings, on the way to the cross, the Transfiguration occurs.

Is the cross so incomprehensible? Modern humanity, having raised so many crosses of its own, surely finds it easier to comprehend the cross upon which humanity hung Jesus. We have concentration camps, racial wars, Hiroshima, Northern Ireland, Vietnam, Iran. Why do the good suffer because of and for the bad? Why are the innocent crushed? Does our sin, corporate or individual sin, extract so awesome a price? Why must the good ones—the Steve Bikos, the Martin Luther Kings—become martyrs? Must the Son of God suffer so that God's will is done? What justice is there in that?

These are questions for which there are no rational answers. Every time the church has attempted to answer the questions of the cross in terms of its theology and doctrine, its efforts have never been completely successful. It is only in worship, in some transfiguring experience of vision, that we come to accept who Christ is and what his chosen way means for him and for us. Understanding is not a requirement for discipleship—Peter's or ours. In worship we see that God is pleased with his Son. We need not understand nor even see clearly the end result of God's pleasure—we are only to listen to him and obey.

The last direct words of God Almighty to the church are these: "This is my beloved Son . . . listen to him." Long before the liturgical year and its seasons, long before Lent, the church must have seen in this story a parable of its worship. The Transfiguration tells us that Christian worship is always on the way to the cross. To the outside observer, the whole endeavor may seem pointless. After all, what difference does it make? What is changed by it all? The Transfiguration on the mountain or, for that matter, the eleven o'clock service on Sunday morning does not eradicate the hard way of discipleship. The cross is still there. The mountaintop does not change that. The world still suffers down in the valley.

On the way to the cross, the church withdraws and listens. It overhears the talk between Jesus, Moses, and Elijah. The shining epiphany comes. The Father confirms the Son's authority. But when it is all over and done with, when the benediction is given and we go forth, nothing seems changed. "Was this only a fantasy trip, an escape from the cares of the world into some mystical world of worship?" we ask.

Here is where Matthew's additional verses (17:6-7) have great meaning. In worship, when the disciples are face to face with God and struck down by fear, Jesus comes, touches them, and says, "Rise and have no fear." Every other occurrence of the word "touch" *(hauptō)* in Matthew is related to *healing.* The fear of the disciples is healed neither by saying that confrontation with God is casual nor by saying there is no reason to fear the way of the cross, but only by Jesus' healing touch, his mystical revelation, and his encouraging word. The work of worship is a healing work.

Richard John Neuhaus, from the vantage point of his inner-city parish in Brooklyn, has seen the vital connection between the healing presence we encounter in worship and the work we do in the world. As far back as his seminary days, says Neuhaus, he had seen that radical service and political action in the world require more than mere humanitarian optimism to sustain them. What was required was

> an intense engagement in the sacramental mystery of The Presence. . . .
> I have observed over the years many ministries in the inner cities of America, and I have witnessed many burned-out cases. Young men and women, and some not so young, who came with admirable devotion and determination to make a difference, but finally the evidence of futility exhausted that devotion and broke that determination. Brooklyn and the South Bronx, and their counterparts . . . , do not deal kindly with those who would change the world for the better. . . .
> Generalizations must be made with care, but I venture this: Where the most difficult ministries are sustained, . . . endurance is empowered by the sacramental anticipation of transcendent hope. Many times people have remarked the frequency with which vital inner-city ministry is joined by a lively emphasis upon liturgy and sacrament. It is no accident.[2]

The worship of the church, in whatever season, is a series of interludes on the way to the cross. Those who worship are also the ones who are on the way of suffering and death. The fear is real. But a divine glory transforms these moments and strengthens us for the hard days ahead. We rise from our worship; we return from the time of withdrawal to resume life in the valley of the shadow of the cross, a valley in which the suffering and pain of the world remain. Worship does not eradicate that suffering of the world, but sometimes worship transfigures the agony. We, like that visionary before us, Martin Luther King, "have been to the mountaintop" and have seen the dream. We go back to the unchanged valley, *ourselves* changed.

The world may think we withdraw to hide, or to escape the pain, or to avoid the cost—sometimes we do. But the world is wrong, dead wrong, if it thinks this is what Christian worship is about. We withdraw in order to return. Without the withdrawal, we probaby could not, would not return. For soon enough, the pain of the world grinds down and wears out the weak ones, the tired ones, the wounded ones. The wounds would bleed us to death were it not for the healing interlude of worship.

We do not always understand what happens in worship or in the world. But mere understanding is not the point. The point is: we withdraw. Then we rise and return, having seen who Jesus really is, having been touched and healed, having been told we need not fear.

8

Blessing:
The Sustaining Presence

2 CORINTHIANS 13:14

The work of worship ends, the last hymn is sung, and the people of God slide their hymnals into the racks while they fumble with gloves, coats, and hats. The pastor stands before the congregation for one last act of worship. The pastor's hands are raised, outstretched over the congregation, as if to embrace, hands pushing out, reaching out from the full sleeves of the black robe. The pastor's eyes move around the congregation, that flock that now prepares to go forth into the world, that world where their work as Christians will continue, where the healing vision must be lived.

There is Sarah Jones in the second pew with the throat cancer that will not heal in spite of her prayers this hour, the man who will not be faithful to his wife in spite of his best intentioned resolutions, the teenager who wants to love and be loved but knows not how, the old woman on the back pew who goes home to two cats and television and cornflakes and loneliness. These are the ones who now look back at their pastor, awaiting the final words before they scatter. Benediction. They await blessing. The pastor speaks,

The grace of our Lord and Savior, Jesus Christ, the love of God, and the fellowship of the Holy Spirit be with you all. Amen.

And they go forth.

A few years ago Paul Pruyser, a Menninger Foundation psychotherapist, sadly noted,

. . . in the American Protestant mainstream, blessing and benediction are not imbued with life. . . . Over the years, in attending worship services, I had gradually become accustomed to ministers' terminating their services with a rushed and hardly audible benediction, uttered on the way out from the back of the sanctuary where nobody could see them. And if the benediction was pronounced from the pulpit, audibly and visibly, the spectacle for the beholders was often little more than a slovenly gesture, consisting of only one arm, raised half-heartedly. . . . [1]

Pruyser laments the demise of this "once powerful and wholesome" symbol of divine providence and presence, this "wonderful pastoral gift."

Why these poor benedictions, this slovenliness in blessing? Why has a once powerful symbolic gesture become an empty formality? Pruyser believes that when pastors sloppily perform a liturgical gesture like a benediction, they are delivering a number of unspoken messages to a congregation: "(1) benedictions are rather meaning-less, (2) the pastor does not deem the people worthy of receiving them, (3) the pastor himself has long given up thoughts of divine providence, or (4) the pastor refuses to shoulder the shepherd's role." [2]

In this final chapter, I hope to restore some meaning to the liturgical act of blessing by an examination of blessing in the New Testament and in the church's worship. [3]

Salvation as Blessing

Claus Westermann notes that the Old Testament and the New Testament agree: God is a God who saves. Our God brings us salvation. The problem is that, for most of us, "salvation" has become a vague, nebulous, religious sounding word without much substance. What does it mean to be saved by this God?

The Greek word for salvation, *sōteria,* signifies an act of deliverance, redemption, liberation. But its Latin counterpart *salus* (from which our word "salvation" is derived) originally meant a state of being "whole," or "healthy." In other words, both the act of deliverance and the state of being delivered are implied in the biblical usage of *sōteria,* or "salvation." In the Bible, to be delivered by God is to have received the blessing of God and vice versa. Salvation is both an act and a state of being.

In recent years theology and biblical interpretation have tended to conceive of God's work among us as a rather sporadic, discontinu-ous, occasional breaking into the flow of our history. This divine punctuation brings "mighty acts" of deliverance and liberation. God is a God who periodically acts to save.

But this view does justice to only one side of the biblical salvation picture. In the Old Testament, not only does God periodically enter history to deliver, redeem, and liberate, but also God shows "steadfast love," "faithfulness from generation to generation." God's grace, in the Bible, is more continuous than recent existentialist and liberation theologies allow. God is present not only in historical deeds but also in daily processes such as birth, death, growth, seedtime and harvest, in day-to-day processes as mundane and unspectacular as sunshine and rain. God is not only the one who says, "I have come down to deliver them" (Exodus 15:21) but is also the God who gives manna in the wilderness and makes Israel to dwell in a land of milk and honey.

Throughout the Old Testament God's blessing—God's continuing, ever-present activity—manifests itself in a number of ways: fertility (Genesis 1:22), power to defeat one's enemies (24:60), and wisdom (Job 12:13). Not only does God the Liberator deliver, but God the Creator and Sustainer also blesses.[4]

It is not possible to limit the workings of God to certain, dramatic, sporadic interventions in history (the tendency of most "prophetic" religion), nor is it possible to confine God to our institutions, culture, and cult alone (the tendency of most "cultic" religion). God is with us in deeds of deliverance as well as in the midst of us as one who is *present.*

Humanly speaking, the act of blessing (*berekah* in the Old Testament) means to impart vital power to another person. When a father blesses his son, he conveys power to him (Genesis 27). When people meet or depart, they bless each other (47:10). "The LORD is with you" (Judges 6:12) is the greeting that makes human relationships possible through the sharing of personal power. This is the *shalom,* both a state of being and an act that makes community. Large public gatherings are concluded with a blessing so that the individual participants may take some of the shared power of the community with them when they depart.

In the Old Testament, worship gatherings are always concluded with a priestly blessing in order that the power of the assembly may go with the individual worshipers as they depart. On occasions such as weddings, just before death, or the beginning of a king's reign, a blessing is given, in word and gesture, as a sign of favor and endowment with power. In fact, the great scholar of the Psalms, Sigmund Morwinckel, flatly declares that, for Israel, the purpose of public worship "is to secure blessing for the community and for the individual."[5]

The LORD said to Moses, "Say to Aaron and his sons, Thus you shall bless the people of Israel: you shall say to them,

> The LORD bless you and keep you:
> The LORD make his face to shine upon
> you, and be gracious to you:
> The LORD lift up his countenance upon
> you, and give you peace.

"So shall they put my name upon the people of Israel, and I will bless them" (Numbers 6:22-27).

Note that in such cultic benedictions the subject of the action, the one who acts to bless, is *God.* God acts through the word and gesture of the priest to bless those who now depart to their homes.

The New Testament builds upon these concepts of blessing with very little modification except to proclaim that Christ is God's blessing (Galatians 3:8-9, 14). Jesus blesses the children (Mark 10:13-16 and parallels). He blesses meals (Mark 6:41 and 8:6-7 and parallels). He pronounces a blessing at the Last Supper (Mark 14:22 and parallels). He blesses his disciples (Luke 24:50-51). Christ not only saves but also blesses. The disciples are told not only to preach but also to bless those whom they meet, even those who curse them (Luke 6:28). In other words, the blessing of God in Christ, given by his disciples, was an integral part of the Christian proclamation and ministry and, in regard to the blessing of enemies, a shocking sign of the radical nature of divine love as seen in the Christ. Here is revelation of God who gives blessing, sends rain on the "just" and even the "unjust" (Matthew 5:45).

In other words, throughout the Old Testament and at numerous crucial points in the New, blessing is not something that is on the periphery, but rather a sign that symbolizes the all-encompassing significance of religion. It is not a petition or prayer, a pious wish for God's presence; it is a statement of faith, a statement of fact. God *is* with you. Nor is blessing some empty formalized gesture that may or may not be effective. It is an effective act that transfers power, a deed that is commanded as an effective sign of God's sustaining presence and present power.

Divine *pronoia* (providence, foresight) enables one to live by faith in the first place. It is an affirmation that God sees beyond our limited comprehension and vision to our ultimate destinies. *Pronoia* is the opposite of cruel, meaningless, uncaring fate. *Pronoia* is an affirmation that God is for us, God is with us.

The trust that this affirmation elicits makes the sustained Christian pilgrimage possible. "If God is for us, who is against us?" (Romans 8:31). Here is trust, not in ourselves, nor trust for the sake of trust, but trust in God without which no courage, no sustained meaning would be possible. The blessing is a visible sign that all of life is undergirded by this trustworthy promise of divine care. *Deus pro nobis*—God for us.

In blessing, Christians continue the Old Testament idea that "salvation," God's saving action in Christ, is not simply a once-and-for-all fact of history that happened once but has no continuing consequences. The presence of God and the sustaining, day-to-day growth, maturity, prosperity, fruitfulness, and well-being that come from that presence—are continued in the New Testament even if the form and mode of that presence are now seen as part of the work of the risen Christ. "Blessed be the God and Father of our Lord Jesus Christ, who has blessed us in Christ with every spiritual blessing in the heavenly places" (Ephesians 1:3).

Worship as Blessing

Christian worship adopted the activity of bestowing a blessing at the conclusion of the assembly, adding to it the sign of the cross.[6] In so doing, the church incorporated all the Old Testament meanings of this act—the steadfast, covenantal love of God; the divine presence even within the most mundane of human activities; the providence of God over his people; God's care for their health and fruitfulness. To these meanings it added its own distinctive coloring—blessing that knows no bounds, even to the point of blessing enemies; blessing of the "least of these," such as children; blessing through healing, thereby showing Christ's care for the well-being of the whole person, a care that is now manifested in the blessing of the Christian community.

Christ's disciples are sent forth (Matthew 10; Luke 10) not merely with a message of the coming kingdom. They also go with a powerful greeting of blessing. The *shalom* of God goes with them. This act of blessing corresponds to the two-fold task of the disciples and the church: preaching and healing. "God be with you."

Blessing as an act of worship within the church takes its meaning from blessing in the Bible. Whether or not the church feels adequate to bless in the name of Christ, whether or not the church's clergy find meaning in this gesture or do it well before their congregations, nevertheless the church stands within this biblical tradition of blessing and bears this commission to bless.

Whenever Christians leave one another, blessing is appropriate. Such blessing at leave-taking is a natural part of everyday life, as natural as shaking hands. We have long ago secularized our leave-taking, but the words we use, even today when we shake hands, point back to blessing. The French *adieu*, the Spanish *adios*, the English "good-bye" are all linguistically derived from "God be with you." They are all human well-wishings that commit another person to the care of God.

Henri Nouwen ponders the significance of our times of leave-taking and calls pastors to be sensitive to the need for "creative withdrawal" in their pastoral work.

> In our ministry of visitation—hospital visits and home visits—it is essential for patients and parishioners to experience that it is good for them, not only that we come but also that we leave. In this way the memory of our visit can become as important, if not more important, than the visit itself. I am deeply convinced that there is a ministry in which our leaving creates space for God's spirit and in which, by our absence, God can become present in a new way. . . . The words of Jesus: "It is for your good that I leave" should be a part of every pastoral call we make. We have to learn to leave so that the Spirit can come. . . . This shows the importance of being sensitive to the last words we speak before we leave a room or house; it also puts the possibility of a prayer before leaving into a new light.[7]

Leave-taking at the end of a service of Christian worship is more significant than our everyday partings because of the nature of the activities which it concludes. In this service we have met and been met by God. We have come into the holy presence of God and the holy presence of the people of God. The blessing is significant as a bridge that joins what happens in worship to what takes place outside. The presence, the sustaining presence, is what beckoned us to this meeting in the first place. That presence made possible any meeting that may have occurred here. That presence becomes blessing enough for those who have come. That presence now goes with these blessed ones as they depart.

The physical gesture of blessing, done with authority, firmness, confidence, as well as audibly and visibly by the pastor in front of the congregation, helps to redeem and transform the ordinary human experience of leave-taking. All of life's myriad of meetings and leave-takings are given new significance when seen as daily opportunities to commit someone to God. On the other hand, the blessing, when restored to the prominence it deserves at the end of the service, reminds us of the human within our divine service. There is little that is "spiritual" about Christian worship—as we often use the term "spiritual" today. Christian worship is not a fantasy trip out of human life, a technique to take you to some ethereal realm of the Spirit. When our God speaks to us, God addresses our total being—our human needs for health, our need for food, for family, friends, jobs, sunshine and rain. The blessing is a gesture that involves the full human being. As such, it directs us to our full range of human needs that God cares about and cares for. The blessing is no magical, sacred bit of archaic priestly mumbo-jumbo. It is a very human, very mundane, very incarnational gesture that expresses the utterly human, mundane, incarnational love of the God who became a man.

The idea of Providence is a bit out of fashion in theological circles these days.[8] Our existentialist and liberation theologies seem embarrassed that the great God should be concerned with something so material and commonplace as rain. Or do we find it even more embarrassing that the great God should stoop to bless one of his children through such poor unworthy folk as we?

A well-done pastoral blessing at the end of a Sunday service may be one way not only to proclaim the reality of Providence to a skeptical church but also to provide the church with firsthand experience of the Master's hand upon their shoulders, blessing them as they go forth. The pastor does in the act of blessing what the pastor often does in the sermon, pastoral counseling sessions, and in the myriad of pastoral encounters that occur in the average congregation: He or she shows to this people that "the Lord is with you." Committing a brother or sister to the Providence of God, sharing the power of the Body of Christ with the individual members of that Body as they scatter, can be a major opportunity for the church to be about its Father's business—the business of blessing.

Thank God, God not only meets us in the mighty saving acts of salvation history but also deigns to meet us in something so close at hand, something so utterly essential and commonplace as rain—or bread, or wine, or children, or good health, or friends.

We are the continual beneficiaries not only of God's salvation but also of God's blessing—and that is our salvation. God's presence among us is a continuous, sustaining, healing, pastoral presence. From Sunday to Sunday, in the week-to-week rhythm of our worship, that presence upholds us. Sometimes our worship is soul shaking and life changing; sometimes it is a time for tears, change, exhilaration and awe that comes when we are brought very close to that presence. But mostly it's just the same—the same hymns, the same preacher, the same church, same children, same wife, same Sunday dinner, same good friends, same rain, same sun, same love, same God. And the fact that it is so ordinary, so expected, so close at hand and so—*same*—is the beauty of it all.

Without the weekly worship, the predictable rhythm, the accustomed ritual of it all, we might forget about the near presence of God. We might wonder if anybody out there cares or is in control. It's the sameness, the steadfastness of it all that makes worship so reassuring, even in the midst of all the uncertainties of life outside the front door of the church. Liturgical experimentation must always proceed with great caution lest we disrupt that steadfast rhythm that is itself a public testimony to the underlying rhythm of steadfast divine care that upholds us.

And while we are giving more attention to extending blessings well, we must also give attention to blessing people more often in worship: a baptism, the Sunday before high school graduation, when a newborn child is brought to church for the first time, when someone confesses sin, when the youth retreat is over, when someone gets married, before someone enters surgery, when a family moves to another town, when someone is near death. Such leave-taking should be named and claimed as appropriate times to do what Christians are called to do and commit someone to the abiding love of God, the sustaining presence.

After all, life being what it is, they'll need it.

God Be with You

And so as the toddlers squirm and Sarah Jones in the second pew clears her throat where her enemy waits, and John Smith grips tightly the hand of the wife to whom he wants to be faithful, and Sue Clardy twirls her finger in her hair and gazes blankly out the open window, and old Miss Thompson sadly rises to her feet; the pastor reaches out, reaches out to the hurt and broken promises, and twisted lives, and unfulfilled dreams, as if to embrace them; gathering them all up for one last tight embrace, gathering unto himself or herself these little ones, gathering them in the name of him who called and loved and blessed the little ones, gathering them in an embrace that encompasses this whole, hurting, world and says in a boldness that at times seems contrary to all the evidence the church sees about it, a boldness born only of faith,

"The grace of the Lord Jesus Christ and the love of God and the fellowship in the Holy Spirit be with you all."

And they go out, and the Sustaining Presence goes with them.

Notes

Chapter 1

[1]James D. Smart, *The Strange Silence of the Bible in the Church: A Study in Hermeneutics* (Philadelphia: The Westminster Press, 1970).

[2]Leander E. Keck, *The Bible in the Pulpit: The Renewal of Biblical Preaching* (Nashville: Abingdon Press, 1978); and D. Moody Smith, *Interpreting the Gospels for Preaching* (Philadelphia: Fortress Press, 1980).

[3]For an example of a new lectionary, see *Seasons of the Gospel,* ed. Hoyt Hickman (Nashville: Abingdon Press, 1979).

[4]See the Proclamation I Series (Philadelphia: Fortress Press, 1973–1978), 26 vols.; Reginald Fuller, *Preaching the New Lectionary* (Collegeville, Minn.: Liturgical Press, 1974); and Gerard Sloyan, *Commentary on the New Lectionary* (New York: Paulist Press, 1975).

[5]See Willi Marxsen, *The New Testament as the Church's Book,* trans. J. E. Mignard (Philadelphia: Fortress Press, 1972).

[6]James F. White, *Christian Worship in Transition* (Nashville: Abingdon Press, 1976), p. 14.

[7]Among the best introductions to worship in the New Testament are: Oscar Cullmann, *Early Christian Worship* (London: SCM Press Ltd., 1953); G. D. Delling, *Worship in the New Testament* (Philadelphia: The Westminster Press, 1962); Ferdinand Hahn, *The Worship of the Early Church,* trans. D. E. Green (Philadelphia: Fortress Press, 1973); and C. F. D. Moule, *Worship in the New Testament* (Richmond: John Knox Press, 1961).

[8]Dom Gregory Dix, *The Shape of the Liturgy* (London: Dacre Press, 1945). See the first two chapters of my book *Word, Water, Wine and Bread* (Valley Forge: Judson Press, 1980) for a more detailed discussion of Jewish and early Christian sacred meals.

[9]C. F. D. Moule, *op. cit.,* p. 8.

Chapter 2

[1]Philip Rieff, *The Triumph of the Therapeutic: Uses of Faith After Freud* (London: Chatto & Windus, 1966), pp. 26-27, 39-41.

Chapter 3

[1]William Meuhl, "The Cult of the Publican," in *All the Damned Angels* (Philadelphia: Pilgrim Press, 1972), pp. 23-31.
[2]Joachim Jeremias, *The Parables of Jesus*, rev. ed. (New York: Charles Scribner's Sons, 1963), p. 140.
[3]*Ibid.*, p. 143.
[4]*Ibid.*
[5]*Ibid.*, p. 141.
[6]See David H. C. Read, *Overheard* (Nashville: Abingdon Press, 1971).

Chapter 4

[1]Portions of this chapter appeared in *Holy Communion* (Nashville: The Graded Press, 1978).
[2]Nahum N. Glatzer, ed., *The Passover Haggadah* (New York: Schocken Books, Inc., 1969), p. 23. Reprinted by permission of Schocken Books, Inc., from *The Passover Haggadah* edited by Nahum N. Glatzer. Copyright © 1953, 1969, 1979 by Schocken Books, Inc.
[3]*Ibid.*, p. 49.
[4]Paul S. Minear, "Some Glimpses of Luke's Sacramental Theology," *Worship*, vol. 44, no. 6 (June-July, 1970), pp. 326-329.

Chapter 5

[1]T. S. Eliot, *The Wasteland* in *The Complete Poems and Plays, 1909–1950* (New York: Harcourt Brace Jovanovich, Inc., 1952), pp. 46-47.
[2]Portions of this chapter are adapted from my work *Remember Who You Are: Baptism, a Model for Christian Life* (Nashville: The Upper Room, 1980).
[3]Quoted in Jean Danielou, S. J., *The Bible and the Liturgy* (Notre Dame, Ind.: University of Notre Dame Press, 1956), pp. 43-44.
[4]Quoted in *ibid.*, pp. 45-46.
[5]David C. Steinmetz, "Reformation and Conversion," *Theology Today*, vol. 35, no. 1 (April, 1978), p. 31.
[6]Juan Carlos Ortiz, *Cry of the Human Heart* (Carol Stream, Ill.: Creation House, 1977), p. 38.

Chapter 6

[1]In my interpretation of Luke 4, I am heavily indebted to James A. Sanders's article, "From Isaiah 61 to Luke 4," in *Christianity, Judaism, and Other Greco-Roman Cults, Part 1: New Testament,* ed. Jacob Neusner (Leiden, The Netherlands: E. J. Brill, 1975), pp. 75-106.
[2]Brevard S. Childs, "The Canonical Shape of the Prophetic Literature," *Interpretation*, vol. 32, no. 1 (January, 1978), p. 55.

Chapter 7

[1]My thanks to Albert Curry Winn's fine article, "Worship as a Healing Experience," *Interpretation*, vol. 29, no. 1 (January, 1975), pp. 68-72, for helping me to organize my exegesis of this passage.
[2]Richard John Neuhaus, *Freedom for Ministry* (New York: Harper & Row, Publishers, Inc., 1979), pp. 95-96.

Chapter 8

[1]Paul W. Pruyser, "The Master Hand: Psychological Notes on Pastoral Blessing," in *The New Shape of Pastoral Theology: Essays in Honor of Seward Hiltner,* ed. William B. Oglesby, Jr. (Nashville: Abingdon Press, 1969), p. 353.

[2]*Ibid.,* p. 361. Elsewhere I have reflected on the consequences of the pastoral blessing for pastoral care and the pastor's identity. See my book *Worship as Pastoral Care* (Nashville: Abingdon Press, 1979), chapter 10.

[3]I am deeply indebted to the fine book on blessing by Claus Westermann, *Der Segen in der Bibel und im Handeln der Kirche,* now in English as *Blessing in the Bible and the Life of the Church,* trans. Keith Crim (Philadelphia: Fortress Press, 1978).

[4]Since such activities as "nurturing" and "sustaining" are carried out in human life predominantly by women (at least in our culture), and because most of our theologians and biblical scholars have been men, I wonder if the neglect of blessing and its counterparts in Scripture is due to a truncated view of human/divine activity held by men. Admittedly, most of the biblical images of divine providence are "masculine": King, Lord, Protector, Provider.

[5]Quoted in Westermann, *op. cit.,* p. 35.

[6]It is interesting that the German word *segnen,* "to bless," is derived from the Latin *signare;* "to make the sign of the cross." This shows the very early relationship between the word and the act of blessing.

[7]Henri J. M. Nouwen, *The Living Reminder* (New York: The Seabury Press, Inc., 1977), pp. 44-45.

[8]For a lucid discussion of the neglect of Providence in theology and a proposal for treatment of the idea through Process Theology, see D. W. D. Shaw, "Providence and Persuasion," *The Duke Divinity School Review,* vol. 45, no. 1 (Winter, 1980), pp. 11-22.

DATE DUE